MW00830128

Praise for *Shine*

"*Shine* is a transformative guide that reminds us that true success begins with self-awareness and inner growth. Gino and Rob's wisdom, combined with real-life stories and practical disciplines, make this book an essential companion for entrepreneurs seeking authentic fulfillment."

—Lewis Howes, host of *The School of Greatness* podcast

"It's possible to be driven and be at complete peace. This book shows you how."

—Dr. Benjamin Hardy, organizational psychologist and author of *10x Is Easier Than 2x*

"Rarely is the inner game of entrepreneurship addressed, and yet it is the ultimate make-or-break determining factor in your success. Gino has already shown us how to master the outer game in his Traction book series, and in *Shine* he and coauthor Rob give you ten disciplines you need to master your inner game and enjoy the process."

—Hal Elrod, internationally bestselling author of *The Miracle Morning*

"What Gino and Rob do in *Shine* is nothing short of spectacular. The inner world of the entrepreneur is a dangerous place to go without a road map and a tool box to navigate a path back out. The ten disciplines are just that. I highly recommend this guide for all my Drivens looking to find freedom from the shame we all carry."

—Douglas Brackmann, PhD, SEP, author of *Driven*

"How do you achieve entrepreneurial freedom? That's what Gino and Rob explore in their new book *Shine*. As a driven entrepreneur, the toll being driven can take on your team, relationships, and well-being is huge. That's why *Shine* gives you ten disciplines for maximizing your energy and impact as an entrepreneur while avoiding burnout. From setting boundaries, to getting into flow, to learning to say no effectively, to thinking in ten-year frames, and a lot more, *Shine* delivers the wisdom and tools you'll need on the journey to entrepreneurial freedom. I highly recommend you read this book!"

—Joe Polish, founder of Genius Network

"Rob and Gino share unique insights about the journey of entrepreneurship, offering wise counsel to those who aspire to be fully conscious as leaders and fully alive as humans."

—Brad Keywell, EY World Entrepreneur of the Year

"An eye-opening journey into the heart of entrepreneurial success. *Shine* brilliantly illustrates that the path to greatness starts from within."

—Jim Dethmer, author of
The 15 Commitments of Conscious Leadership

SHINE

SHINE

HOW LOOKING INWARD IS THE KEY TO UNLOCKING TRUE ENTREPRENEURIAL FREEDOM

10 Disciplines for Maximizing Your
Energy, Impact, and Inner Peace

GINO WICKMAN
AND **ROB DUBE**

BenBella Books, Inc.
Dallas, TX

EOS®, The Entrepreneurial Operating System®, and EOS Implementer® are all registered trademarks of EOS Worldwide, LLC.

BenBella Books, Inc.
10440 N. Central Expressway
Suite 800
Dallas, TX 75231
benbellabooks.com
Send feedback to feedback@benbellabooks.com

BenBella is a federally registered trademark.

Printed in the United States of America
10 9 8 7 6 5 4 3 2 1

Library of Congress Control Number: 2023046629
ISBN 9781637745144 (print)
ISBN 9781637745151 (ebook)

Copyediting by James Fraleigh
Proofreading by Ashley Casteel and Sarah Vostok
Text design and composition by PerfecType, Nashville, TN
Illustrations by Ralph Voltz
Cover design by Ty Nowicki
Printed by Lake Book Manufacturing

To Kathy, for your support, intuition,
strength, and helping me listen
to my True Self every time my ego tried to stop me. I love you.
—Gino Wickman

To the love of my life, Emily, and our children,
William and Frances. I love you more than words
can describe.
—Rob Dube

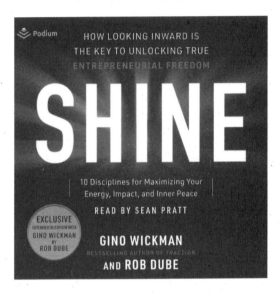

CONTENTS

FINDING YOUR TRUE SELF

Most driven entrepreneurs Rob and I know demonstrate an intense passion for their vision along with a relentless commitment to success. This intensity is a powerful contributor to business triumphs, but it often comes from a dark source, such as childhood trauma, past wounding, fear, depression, or anxiety. As a result, many entrepreneurs achieve significant business success only to find inner satisfaction elusive. The darkness that drove them to achieve so much never seems to go away.

I have helped tens of thousands of entrepreneurs achieve significant business success by using a disciplined and practical approach to operating their businesses. Yet I have come to learn that there are disciplines and a practical approach to accomplish significant *life* success, as well.

Entrepreneurs can use the methods in this book to find a way to free their True Selves and achieve inner peace. With this peace comes a new level of energy and effectiveness. No longer will the darkness that drove you to success get in the way of enjoying your achievements. It is possible to be driven *and* have inner peace. You *can* truly shine once you find and free your True Self.

People have an outer world story and an inner world story, and typically they are very different. I'd like to share both of mine, in the hopes that they likewise will inspire you to shine.

My Outer World Story

I grew up as a rebellious entrepreneur-in-the-making, always finding ways to make money. I barely graduated high school with a solid 2.3 GPA. As my friends went off to college, I stayed home and got a job. I wanted to work and make money. I set a goal for myself that I would be earning $50,000 by age twenty-five (that was a lot in 1985). I worked in a machine shop, sold corporate travel, and invested in real estate. By age twenty-three I had made twice my goal in real estate sales.

The next year, I joined the family business my dad had founded, which had become the number-one real estate sales-training company in North America. I worked my way from the bottom to the top in fourteen months, going from product sales, to product sales manager, to vice president of client relations, to being a member of the executive committee, to president of the company. At age twenty-five, as part of the executive committee, I quickly learned that the family business was deep in debt and needed a turnaround. I believed I could save it and met with my dad to share my plan. He handed me the keys to the business and a personal check for $100,000 (to pay some critical bills and make payroll), and I went to work.

I turned the business around in three years, paying off all of its debt and getting it profitable and growing again. I ran it for a few more years while becoming a one-third owner of the business, then we decided to sell it. After the sale I stayed on for a year to transition in the new leadership team, and I retired from the company at thirty-one.

I then set off to pursue what I realized was my true passion: helping entrepreneurs get everything they want from their business and life. I found one client, then another, and then another. They started referring me to their friends.

Over five years, I honed, refined, and tested countless ideas, theories, and methodologies while delivering five hundred full-day sessions with fifty companies. I also put the finishing touches on what the world now knows as EOS, The Entrepreneurial Operating System. Today, more than two hundred thousand driven entrepreneurs all over the world are using EOS to run better companies. I have also written seven other books that have sold more than two million copies.

Over the last thirty years, I have created four practical methodologies that have helped hundreds of thousands of driven entrepreneurs live their ideal *outer* life. They address every aspect of the entrepreneur's climb:

1. I created *Entrepreneurial Leap* to help anyone who thinks they want to be an entrepreneur discover if they are and to show them a path to becoming incredibly successful. I lived this content firsthand as an eighteen-year-old

misfit who had no idea what I was, only to discover, at twenty-nine, that I was an entrepreneur.

2. I created *Rocket Fuel* to help Visionary entrepreneurs on their journey and determine when it is time to find their ideal Integrator counterpart (president/COO) to run the day-to-day of their business and help take the company to the next level. I lived this content firsthand, serving as the Integrator to my Visionary father for seven years while running the family business. Then I became the Visionary to my amazing Integrator partner, Don Tinney, while founding EOS Worldwide, growing it 40 percent per year for ten years, and then selling it.

3. I created The Entrepreneurial Operating System (EOS) to guide entrepreneurs in running their business like a Swiss watch. As I mentioned, more than two hundred thousand entrepreneurs use the EOS tools in *Traction* (the how-to book for implementing EOS). We ran EOS Worldwide on EOS while helping all of my clients do the same.

4. In addition, I created *The EOS Life* to help an entrepreneur live their ideal life by giving them the tools to spend every day doing what they love, with people they love, making a huge difference, being compensated appropriately, with time for other passions. This content was developed from my experience of running the family business and building EOS Worldwide. I have been living The EOS Life for twenty-five years.

I have a great family and friends whom I love deeply and who I believe love me, and I have every material possession I'll ever need. In addition, I have had a pretty good work–life balance. For the last twenty years, I have taken 150 days off per year, including an annual August sabbatical. By any measure, my *outer* world story has been pretty good.

My Inner World Story

Beneath the surface, however, I grew up with a lot of pain and trauma. At both six and seven, I was sexually abused by an older boy in the neighborhood. Those two experiences really screwed me up. I always felt so much shame.

I sucked my thumb in private until I was eight years old. It was probably a safety issue. I was always embarrassed about that.

My family moved nine times by the time I was ten years old (entrepreneurial dad), so I never felt settled.

I was a tiny, highly sensitive, creative kid who was picked on and bullied until I was fourteen, which led me to feel unsafe and become very angry in my late teens. Growing up, I felt like I had to prove to the world, and to myself, that there was nothing wrong with me. That I was okay.

At age fifteen, alcohol touched my lips for the first time. While it didn't become an addiction, it numbed my pain. It changed the way I saw myself and the world. I learned how to create a tough guy facade, push my sadness under my anger, and build layers of armor to protect myself from the world, while shielding and burying my pain. I spent the next seven years working, drinking, and fighting.

During that phase, my ego created the perfect go-getter persona. Besides never feeling that pain again, I accomplished everything I *thought* I wanted over the next thirty-five years.

I went broke three times, at ages twenty-one, twenty-five, and thirty-three. The last was the worst. I achieved my goal of becoming a millionaire at thirty-one. Then I went broke and was $200,000 in debt by thirty-three, with a $150,000-per-year life-style, a wife, and a five- and an eight-year-old. I had lost $1.4 million in two years due to bad investments, risk-taking, and poor planning. I felt like such a failure, and the stress almost killed me.

I thought it was normal to go through life feeling uneasy, anxious, and depressed. I didn't think of it as pain; I thought everyone felt that way.

At age forty-five, I learned from my doctor after a calcium scan that I had damaged one of my heart valves due to the extreme stress of working nonstop in my twenties.

Shoot forward to one day at age fifty-two, a couple of years after selling EOS Worldwide. That day, I was celebrating my life. Besides the company, I had sold over a million books. I also had more than a hundred thousand companies using the tools I created, an amazing family and friends, and all the material stuff and accolades of success. I'd made it to the top of the mountain.

I'm embarrassed to say this but, at that moment, I literally thought I was perfect.

Immediately after that thought, the universe hit me over the head with a sledgehammer.

I can only describe it as an awakening. I was forced to look inside, and when I did, all I felt was pain. An extreme feeling of emptiness, yearning, and sadness. I realized that, despite the mountain I had climbed, all that outer stuff hadn't filled the hole inside me.

As I explored this feeling over the next few years, trying to understand it, a wellspring of emotions erupted. I experienced full-blown the pain and trauma I had stuffed down for so many decades.

I realized how few times I had been truly present with my kids and my wife. The discovery broke my heart. Here I was, taking time off, being home by six o'clock most workdays, and living a "balanced" life. Meanwhile, I was a zombie with my family, thinking about everything else but them. I was physically present, but my mind was in a million other places. It's painful to recount.

I also realized that because of my childhood experiences, I had always felt ashamed, lonely, and unsafe, constantly having to prove to myself and others that I was okay. I didn't feel people's love. I felt I was never enough for them. I feared failure, feared judgment.

All those years, I was in denial. I was in a prison created by my own ego, and I didn't know what to do about it. I didn't even know what shame meant before this awakening. My True Self was not free.

You may be able to relate to some of this.

Life had more in store for me during these years of awakening. I almost died three times within twelve months. I was caught in a gas explosion in my home caused by a leak that went right into my office. My brakes went out at eighty miles per hour on a highway exit ramp while approaching an intersection—thank God I found the emergency brake. And COVID almost killed me due to my stupidity after I French-kissed my wife when she came home after testing positive. I wanted to catch COVID and get it over with, but the viral overload gave me double pneumonia, and my blood oxygen level dropped into the low seventies. I could barely climb stairs, yet I refused to go to the hospital.

I'm not telling my inner world story looking for a pity party. Nor am I sharing my trauma so the world can feel sorry for me. I have no interest in being a victim; I don't feel like one at all. Rather, I'm sharing my inner story to release all this turmoil. To set it free. To set *me* free. And to help you do the same.

There is such power and freedom in sharing your inner story. I urge you to write yours down right now.

_____

_____

_____

_____

_____

_____

_____

_____

_____

_____

_____

_____

_____

_____

_____

_____

_____

_____

_____

_____

As I created the four methodologies for driven entrepreneurs, I masked my inner pain and emptiness through sheer will, my drive to become successful, and my ability to put on a good face. I was masterful at helping entrepreneurs build empires. Only later did I realize that what I was doing for my clients, I had done for myself: built an amazing outer world that ignored inner pain and emptiness. So what does that mean now? It's time to turn the good parts of your drive to all aspects of your life.

Why This Book?

I am writing this book (in this case, with my coauthor, Rob Dube), as I have written all of my books, to help entrepreneurs. I have traveled the same road—and found it incomplete. In the same way I have helped others through practical methods of helping them grow their business, I have learned methods that can allow you to flourish internally in ways you never expected.

I am also writing because, as I shared my story with others, I learned that I am not alone in my experience.

Ron Harrell, founder and CEO of My Office, which provides office furniture solutions, built a business, sold it, and had two children, a loving family, a nice new home, and a fun, adventurous life, all by the age of forty. That was Ron's outer world story. His inner world story was much different. Because of the energy and focus he had put into his business, his marriage was a mess. He started to realize that he had a lot of anger and negative self-judgment, and was unable to love deeply or have loving relationships with anyone, including his wife and daughters. Ron's struggle to fully open his heart and feel deeply led to a divorce. While he still had a lot of outer world fun in his life, he was simply masking his inner pain, leading him to a crash. This crash was his wake-up call to begin doing inner work and start feeling peace, love, and joy in his life.

Mark O'Donnell, Visionary at EOS Worldwide, had early success in his entrepreneurial career. His businesses won big projects and, at one point, he had three companies on the *Inc.* 5000 list, one company making that list five times. That was his *outer world* success. His *inner world* story was that his wife was carrying 100 percent of the burden at home, had three miscarriages, and coped alone with the final loss while he was taking a partner trip to Germany to grow the company further. Mark's obsession left a wake of destruction that was rarely visible to the outside world. That has all changed with the inner work he has done over the last five years.

Eric Rieger, a client of The 10 Disciplines Coaching Program and True Self Mastermind, and CEO of WEBIT Services, an IT services and consulting company, had experienced great success. At one point his company was recognized by *Forbes* as one of America's Small Giants. That was his *outer world* success. His *inner world* story is that as a child, he was bullied and became a loner. His active imagination would create worlds to which he would escape. Eric's father was a truck driver and his mother worked part-time at various jobs. While his father was a giving person who always put others before himself, his mother was a narcissist who only took an active role in family life when something went wrong, at which point she would forcefully point out everyone's flaws. His father would be gone for five or six days at a time, which Eric later learned was "runaway" behavior. Eric followed suit: whenever anything in his life got difficult, he would bury himself in his business. In 2018, Eric became extremely depressed and would go to bed every night praying he wouldn't wake up the next morning. He now loves life and is even more driven to make a bigger impact.

Ron, Mark, and Eric's stories have improved dramatically because they spent time on their inner world. You'll learn more about how to do so as you read on.

Imagine being your True Self, having substantially more energy, creativity, productivity, impact, peace, joy, and fulfillment than you do right now. Imagine shining bright and being totally free of what is blocking you.

I am happy to say that, after my wakeup call, in the last four years I have experienced more peace, joy, and fulfillment than in my previous fifty-two. I'm also more driven and motivated to make an even bigger impact on the world than ever before. I feel I'm finally my True Self. And I want that for you.

My hope is that this book will catch you before you get to the top of your entrepreneurial mountain, so you can enjoy the climb. If you've made it to the top already, that's okay. Now is your time to enjoy it. And my ultimate hope for every driven entrepreneur is that you realize, as I did, that there *is* no mountain. It's all a journey.

As we get to work, I would like to offer a disclaimer that this is not a mental health book. Rob and I are not psychologists, therapists, or psychiatrists. This book focuses on performance, personal development, and self-mastery. You'll learn to shed your "stuff" so you can have more joy, fulfillment, and peace while being more productive, effective, and impactful.

It's also important to note that this is not a spiritual or religious book. Our clients come from all walks of life. Some are devout in their religion, some are very spiritual. Some are atheists. This book is about finding, freeing, and fully being your True Self, whatever your beliefs or background.

You are going to learn ten powerful disciplines that will maximize your freedom, energy, creativity, impact, and inner peace. They will help you succeed in your outer world *and* your inner world. These 10 Disciplines have evolved greatly over the past few years. I created them when delivering a keynote speech and simply wanted to share with the audience ten things that have greatly impacted my success. The response was so overwhelming, I started teaching them and then included them in two of my previous books and a free eBook.

The difference is, in those books The 10 Disciplines focused on your outer world. When I first created them, I didn't anticipate the robust impact they would have and how they would evolve, so I covered them in just a handful of pages. Nor had I expected them to help people free their True Selves and have greater inner peace. What you are about to read is their full evolution. This expanded version is designed to have an incredible impact on your inner world as well as your outer world.

Before we help you fully implement The 10 Disciplines, Rob and I will introduce you to The 3 Discoveries to Free Your True Self, which both create the context and help you understand the end game when you apply The 10 Disciplines to your life:

- In Discovery #1, you'll learn to embrace that you are driven.
- In Discovery #2, you'll realize decisions are made out of love or fear.
- And in Discovery #3, you'll see that it is possible to be driven *and* have peace.

Again, we start with those 3 Discoveries so that you understand what the outcome of implementing The 10 Disciplines in your life will be—what it feels like to be free.

Then, once you fully understand *what* The 3 Discoveries mean, we get to work on *how* to free your True Self through The 10 Disciplines.

When we get to The 10 Disciplines, we will teach you how they can lay a foundation that creates space in your busy life for you to consistently do this inner work. These disciplines are simple and powerful. You will learn how to adopt the following strategies and behaviors:

1. 10-Year Thinking
2. Take Time Off
3. Know Thyself
4. Be Still
5. Know Your 100%
6. Say No . . . Often
7. Don't Do $25-an-Hour Work
8. Prepare Every Night
9. Put Everything in One Place
10. Be Humble

What you will see by the end of this book is how to live with a harmonious combination of being highly impactful, while experiencing an incredible sense of inner peace. We call this state being in Flowt™, which is a combination of two words, "flow" and "float." You are in the *flow* when you are working and you feel like you are in the zone; time slows down, and you are performing at your best. At the same time you will *float* through all aspects of your life with a feeling of serenity, calm, fulfillment, and ease, comfortably letting your freak flag fly. We will show you how to experience total freedom from your mind, ego, and pain, while maximizing your energy, being incredibly creative, having a lot more fun, and making an even greater impact on the world.

The True Self Exercise

To help you see where you are now, let's start with this exercise.

Please close your eyes, take three slow breaths, and picture yourself and your entire life.

Now remove from your life your business . . . your employees . . . your accolades . . . your accomplishments . . . your family . . . your friends . . . your addictions . . . your hobbies . . . your money . . . your house . . . and your goals.

What is left?

You.

Only you. Completely alone, with nothing but yourself.

Please sit with that for a minute.

How do you feel? Do you feel lonely, uncomfortable, or scared? Or do you feel joy, unconditional self-love, and self-trust?

Whenever I do this exercise with people, they range somewhere between feeling pain or peace.

Lynn Rousseau, CEO of The Conscious Leader, which provides executive leadership coaching for individuals and teams, found that while doing this exercise, she felt her True Self—a calm, clear, wise, and loving presence. This was followed by sadness and regret because she doesn't always make space for her True Self. Lynn said, "It is naturally present and in the forefront when I'm with clients. Even though I can feel the power in this core part of me, it gets pushed aside with the busyness of my workdays, weeks, and months. I feel a deep longing to 'be' with this part of me and to allow it to have more airtime, to be in the driver's seat."

Joseph, one of our clients, shared his belief that fear is what drove him to excel. This realization came during the True Self Exercise. After mentally removing everything from his life, with eyes closed, he shared that it felt so "terrifying," he had the urge to open his eyes during it. He then began to feel "under-enlightened" because of that awareness. Being driven seemed like a blessing, and being surrounded by other entrepreneurs made it feel normal. He realized that pressure and fear drove his tendency, with his businesses, to see how long he could hang by his fingertips on the edge of a cliff until he was about to fall, or how quickly he could get the bank account close to $0 and then be motivated to get back to work again. Joseph thought his superpower was being able to live on the edge but always bringing himself back.

When Nate Klemp, a founding partner of Mindful, a comprehensive media platform for mindfulness and mental health, took the exercise, he found it to be "so powerful to see all of these layers that ordinarily define me fall away." He could see how attached he was to labels, credentials, and other status markers.

We've led numerous groups through this exercise, and I am in awe of the inspiring feedback we receive every time.

If you, like me, have experienced pain for so many years, you will do anything to avoid ever feeling that pain again. You may bury it deep and avoid looking inside. Yet the pain shows up in many little ways, in all aspects of your life. It's always there. It could govern how you treat your spouse, whether that shows up as jealousy, control, manipulation, neediness, feeling unworthy, or anger. It could show up with your employees as a need for recognition, shouting, judgment, micromanagement, or feeling out of control. Or, it could rule your decisions, running them all through an ego filter, trying to anticipate everyone's reaction and judgment despite the fact that you know the right thing to do. The pain distracts you from making the best decisions—with your business plans, your employees, and those you love. You are not fully you.

But when you free your True Self, you will feel peace.

I'm going to introduce you to a new kind of fuel. You may have lived your life, as I did, fueled by outer motivators—fear, revenge for old wounds, achieving goals, competition, trying to prove you're good enough. It is now time to shift to a fuel that is more powerful, from motivators inside you—following your calling, your intuition, your soul's desire, love, and listening to your True Self.

My Coauthor

I've mentioned my coauthor, Rob Dube, but now I would like to formally and proudly introduce him. I am blessed to call Rob a friend. He is a successful entrepreneur, author, podcaster, and family man. As I share my personal examples in this book, he will do the same, along with stories from our clients and many others who were ready to take this natural next step. Rob and I will be writing this book from my voice. When I'm sharing Rob's advice or story, I will say, "Rob says." We both feel this will provide readers the best flow.

I met Rob more than twenty years ago. He and his business partner, Joel Pearlman, are the founders of imageOne, one of my first EOS clients. They embraced the process and mastered it. Within five years, the two sold their business to a public company and then, eighteen months after that, bought it back. He's also an accomplished runner who has completed fourteen marathons, qualifying for the prestigious Boston Marathon five times—including the year of the bombing. Fortunately, he finished forty-five minutes before the blast, but he witnessed the terror live from his hotel room window.

Rob's inner world story goes like this. At age eight, his world was disrupted, first by his parents' divorce, then by severe health issues and mental, physical, and sexual abuse. By coincidence, Rob also sucked his thumb until age eight too; we discovered this while writing the book together. After his parents' divorce, Rob found solace in sports, spending hours hitting and throwing a tennis ball against the wall of his childhood home. He also played imaginary games and conversed with imaginary friends.

Although he didn't like peanut butter, his mom would make him peanut butter and jelly sandwiches, telling him she didn't know any kid who didn't like them. The sandwiches made him sick, but he felt odd that he wasn't like everyone else. It turned out he was allergic to peanut butter. At a routine dentist appointment, it was discovered that the breathing and wheezing he was experiencing was asthma. He was placed on prednisone, which left him jittery and uneasy, and his mom would try to calm his asthma attacks with shots of whiskey. Entering high school, he was four feet, eight inches tall and was teased and bullied constantly. At age fifteen, during an asthma attack, he literally gave up on life and nearly died. Fortunately, his father came home in time to get him the help he needed.

By the age of twenty-two, Rob had started imageOne with Joel and gotten married. By age twenty-five, he and his wife had had their first child. Less than a year later, he noticed he wasn't as good of a person as he wanted to be. He was depressed, not present, consistently anxious about everything, and had obsessive-compulsive disorder. Rob began his healing by going to traditional talk therapy and practicing meditation to help manage his neuroses. In addition, he used such resources as energy healers, acupuncture, Reiki therapy, plant medicine, journaling, gratitude, annual silent retreats, and sweat lodges. Through the work Rob has done, he has freed his True Self and is making a bigger impact and enjoying peace daily. While life is always a work in progress, he experiences much more joy compared to twenty-five years ago.

Rob and I joined forces on this very important work when he approached me after learning The 10 Disciplines and saw the impact they were having. We went to lunch and he said, "I want to help you take The 10 Disciplines to the world." Today, in addition to running the company, Rob facilitates all of our Group Coaching. It is his superpower.

Our goal with this book is to ping your soul, lift the veil, and flip the way you've been functioning and how you see the world. To get a sense of where you are right now, please think of a spectrum. On the far left end are people who might be feeling empty, unfulfilled, lonely, or in pain. Sadly, this is the state of most driven entrepreneurs who have succeeded in the outer world. On the rightmost end of the spectrum are those who have mastered their inner world and feel whole and complete, fulfilled, and peaceful, along with enjoying their many accomplishments.

Put a hash mark on the line where you feel you are on this spectrum. That is your starting point.

Pain   Peace
Empty   Joy
Unfulfilled ├─────────────────────────────┤ Fulfillment
Sad   Love
Lonely   Connected

Wherever you are right now, it's okay. That's your starting point. You are right where you need to be. The process, from here, is to keep moving the needle toward inner peace. Where you fully know yourself so you can be yourself. Where you are 100% you in every situation and completely joyful. Where your True Self is free and you are totally unrestricted, bringing the best version of yourself to everything in your life. The process is actually simple: you are going to remove everything that isn't you, everything holding you back.

Driven entrepreneurs are producers. We work. We practice our craft and create value. This book will show you how to do that even better. You will realize a balance between having renewed energy and more creativity, making a heightened impact, and feeling a new level of peace.

We summarize all of this with two simple words: impact and peace.

Impact includes being creative, applying your craft, being productive, providing value, doing, and serving people.

Peace encompasses trusting yourself, radiating positive energy, joy, feeling connected to everything, unconditionally loving yourself and others, and trusting your intuition.

As a driven entrepreneur, you typically have the productive part down. You have enough brute force to succeed. You're just not experiencing a lot of peace and, therefore, you are not making as big an impact as you could.

Please take our True Self Assessment before reading on to determine where you are on your journey. You will take it again at the end of this book to see how you've progressed. You can also take it at The10Disciplines.com/book.

THE TRUE SELF ASSESSMENT

Read each of the following statements and rank yourself 1–5, where 1 is "not true" and 5 is "100% true."

		1	2	3	4	5
1.	In all of my decisions, thoughts, and actions, I have at least a ten-year time frame in mind.	❑	❑	❑	❑	❑
2.	I spend enough time away from work to rest and reset my energy and clarity levels.	❑	❑	❑	❑	❑
3.	I am comfortable and confident being my True Self in every personal and professional situation.	❑	❑	❑	❑	❑
4.	I consistently practice stillness to create space and clarity in my life.	❑	❑	❑	❑	❑
5.	I know the perfect amount of hours per day and weeks per year during which I want to deliver my value to the world.	❑	❑	❑	❑	❑
6.	I know when to say no, to say no often, and to set effective boundaries.	❑	❑	❑	❑	❑
7.	I know my superpower and delegate all the work that competes with my productivity and drains my energy.	❑	❑	❑	❑	❑
8.	I end every day with a plan in place for tomorrow.	❑	❑	❑	❑	❑
9.	I am organized, consistent, and never drop the ball on promises or commitments made to others.	❑	❑	❑	❑	❑
10.	I practice empathy toward, view myself as equal to, and respect everyone I encounter.	❑	❑	❑	❑	❑

11. I have worked through all past trauma and left behind all feelings of anxiety, shame, or depression. ❑ ❑ ❑ ❑ ❑

12. I am aware of the ways my drive is a blessing and a curse. ❑ ❑ ❑ ❑ ❑

13. I completely understand that I am made up of pure energy and know when my energy is blocked. ❑ ❑ ❑ ❑ ❑

14. I am aware of my pain/trauma and can remove the associated blocked energy preventing me from experiencing peace. ❑ ❑ ❑ ❑ ❑

15. I am aware of and connected to my True Self. ❑ ❑ ❑ ❑ ❑

16. I know when I am making decisions out of love or fear. ❑ ❑ ❑ ❑ ❑

17. I am fully present, aware, and connected to the people around me at every moment. ❑ ❑ ❑ ❑ ❑

18. I am making the impact I want in the world. ❑ ❑ ❑ ❑ ❑

19. I feel a sense of peace, joy, fulfillment, and bliss in my life. ❑ ❑ ❑ ❑ ❑

20. I am completely free to be my True Self always. ❑ ❑ ❑ ❑ ❑

Total number of each ranking ❑ ❑ ❑ ❑ ❑

x1 x2 x3 x4 x5

Multiply by the number above ❑ ❑ ❑ ❑ ❑

Add all five numbers to determine the percentage score that reflects you being your True Self.

_____%

As you see your result, we invite you to reflect on what you are most proud of and grateful for at this point in your life. What will you be able to do to strengthen the areas of the assessment where you did not score as high as you would have liked? Before you continue reading, write down your thoughts in the space below:

_____

_____

_____

_____

_____

_____

_____

_____

_____

_____

_____

_____

_____

_____

_____

_____

_____

_____

THE 3 DISCOVERIES TO FREE YOUR TRUE SELF

In the next three chapters, we will be teaching you 3 Discoveries that will help you free your True Self. You are about to start on a path to free yourself, shed your pain, and have incredible joy. That will set the stage for The 10 Disciplines, which create the foundation to do the work and enable you to maximize both your outer world and inner world success and mastery.

The number-one objective of reading The 3 Discoveries is awareness. The 3 Discoveries are intended to introduce you to your True Self. They will help you understand the context of freeing that self. Once you understand them, you can start implementing The 10 Disciplines in your life. If you are looking for something to "do" while reading and understanding these Discoveries, you might get frustrated. Just keep in mind that

The 3 Discoveries are the "what," and The 10 Disciplines are the "how."

These next three chapters are based on three revelations made over the last five years that have been incredibly freeing for me, Rob, and our clients. I hope they do the same for you.

Many ask why we teach The 3 Discoveries first and The 10 Disciplines second. Why not reverse it? Simple: because we want to begin at the end. We want to show what is possible if you implement The 10 Disciplines in your life . . . to prepare you for what will come up as a result of implementing them.

Before we dive into The 3 Discoveries, please review the following model. It will greatly help you understand and anchor the context of what you are about to read. The 3 Discoveries go deep, and without a big-picture understanding of the model going in, some readers get lost, confused, or overwhelmed.

The 3 Discoveries Model

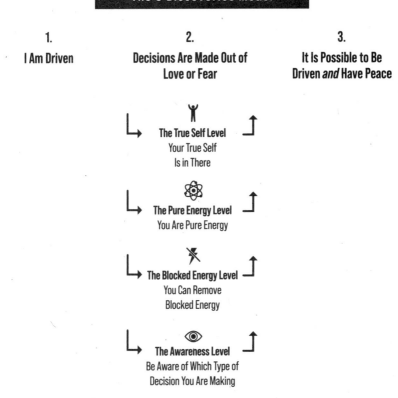

1.

I Am Driven

2.

Decisions Are Made Out of Love or Fear

3.

It Is Possible to Be Driven *and* Have Peace

The True Self Level
Your True Self
Is in There

The Pure Energy Level
You Are Pure Energy

The Blocked Energy Level
You Can Remove
Blocked Energy

The Awareness Level
Be Aware of Which Type of
Decision You Are Making

I AM DRIVEN

This book is for driven entrepreneurs. If you've made it to this point, you must be driven. To fully realize your potential, it is important to understand what it means to be driven—both the good and the bad. Once I understood all the facets of being driven, I felt a thousand pounds lighter. I finally understood myself. I felt complete.

Being driven means you have an internal fire that burns strongly. You have a sense of urgency, a sense that you must do it (whatever "it" is) now, as time is running out!

You are incredibly competitive and want to succeed. Losing is not an option. You want to win, and when you lose, it eats at your insides. It also stokes that internal fire and motivates you to persevere and get better.

You are self-motivated and love to hustle. You will outwork anyone and do whatever it takes to succeed. You have always been the hardest worker in anything you have done. It's natural to you, even though most people don't understand why you work so hard.

Yet, being driven is a blessing and a curse.

On the plus side, when there's a problem, people call on you. You are a superhero; you save the day. You are blessed with superhuman stamina and can endure more than most. Driven people like you have ambition, passion, and a relentless pursuit of goals that fuel the world's innovation and progress. You are the creators, the builders.

Unfortunately, these intense gifts can cause great damage to you and those around you. Damage to your body, your energy, your psyche, and your mind, as well as to relationships with your family, friends, and coworkers. Because nothing ever seems good enough, your restlessness can leave a burnt trail of strained or failed relationships and businesses behind you.

The fuel that charges you comes primarily from outer world motivators and measurement. Driven entrepreneurs often compare themselves to people in their life like their parents, siblings, competitors, friends, or neighbors. They want to prove they are at least as successful as those people.

All your success should be applauded. It has gotten you this far, all driven by outer world factors. Yet you may not be aware of a new and more powerful fuel source you can access—one that comes from the inside. When you combine your outer world skills with this new inner world fuel, you will truly be a force of nature.

Driven by DNA

This driven part of you is coursing through your blood. We all have genes for two particular dopamine receptors in the brain, D2 and D4, but they manifest differently in driven people. In his book *Driven: Understanding and Harnessing the Genetic Gifts Shared by Entrepreneurs, Navy SEALs, Pro Athletes, and Maybe YOU*, Douglas Brackmann, PhD, explains that approximately 10 percent of the population has an "allele, or mutation that changes the number of receptors on the D2/D4 receptor sites, as well as the way dopamine is transported between the cells to these reward centers in the brain." Because of this, the D2/D4 receptors do not fire as easily, making it harder for driven people to feel rewarded and, consequently, either successful or satisfied.

Brackmann writes that all of this can "lead you to feel there is something wrong with you, and the associated shame can create a hellish existence." Further, "the driven are at risk for addictions they believe will provide relief," because they "are innately pulled toward the success they believe will finally leave them feeling rewarded."

He also states, in the words of the driven, "I am different. I am wired to feel like I'm never enough or it's never enough, and I'm always looking for something better." If you can relate to what Brackmann writes, then you probably are driven.

In my thirty-plus years of working with driven entrepreneurs, I have learned that most of those who have realized a high level of outer world success still feel empty as a result. This includes people such as Jillian Lorenz, cofounder and CEO of the Barre Code Fitness franchise, a national group-fitness program engineered for women. From an outer world view, Jillian was living the dream, having grown a $20,000 investment into a multimillion-dollar enterprise. She had a loving husband and four beautiful children. Yet she couldn't understand why she felt an internal void when all of her outer world goals were met. The void led her to begin her inner work journey. Over several years of reading, breathwork, meditation, talk therapy, and journaling, she realized that nothing could overshadow the lack of love she had for herself. It would haunt her until she did the work to accept herself.

Sometimes this sense of being different comes from feeling like an alien. I always felt that way. I worked my ass off, outworking most of my coworkers, for almost forty years. Starting with that machine shop at age eighteen, where I was a gear hobber (using cutting tools to make gear teeth), I was obsessed with being the most efficient worker there, laboring as many hours and running as many machines as I could. My fellow shop workers didn't really like that I worked so hard, although the owner loved me. Following that, I became a top real estate agent, selling over $5 million in my second year in business (with an average sale price of $137,000). I remember many of my fellow agents were resentful. I then took over running and co-owning my family's real estate sales training company in my twenties.

All of that doesn't happen to young people too often, so I didn't have any peers my age who knew what I was going through. Likewise, at family and friend gatherings, I did not enjoy most of the conversations. I felt so out of place. But when the conversation turned to business or someone suggested a competitive game to play, I lit up!

Maybe you can relate to this "feeling like an alien" experience.

Going Through the Motions

The driven are typically not fully present with the people they love. "Present" means you are focused and engaged in the here and now, not distracted, mentally absent, or drifting. Your mind is always racing, thinking, solving. Think about how this affects your relationships. How unimportant it makes people feel. This includes forgetting birthdays and anniversaries, showing up late for important family events, and, when at the event, being there in body only.

Brett Kaufman, founder of Kaufman Development, a real estate development company, feels internal pain when he thinks about the times he has not been present with his son: "On multiple occasions, he has said to me, 'Dad, did you hear me?'"

Mark O'Donnell has a similar story. "I have so many examples of my kids saying, 'Can you play with me?' and me saying no because I was either exhausted from the day, or actively thinking about a problem or opportunity I wanted to solve. It is painful to think about all those times and how it now manifests itself. Eventually, my son stopped asking. He got the brunt of my entrepreneurial career. My first daughter was already born before I started my company, and my second daughter was born after the business was already successful. I had more freedom and a focus on having more balance. I was still distracted from time to time with her but was aware of what I was doing. With my son, I had no idea what I was doing and the impact my mental checkout was having."

Brett and Mark's stories are not unique, as many driven entrepreneurs are consistently distracted, leading to strained relationships with family and friends.

Numbing the Pain

Justin Breen, CEO of BrEpic Communications LLC and author of the book *Epic Life: How to Build Collaborative Global Companies While Putting Your Loved Ones First*, wrote an *Inc.* magazine article addressing common wounds that entrepreneurs have experienced. He states, "I have yet to meet an entrepreneur who hasn't experienced at least one of the following:

1. Bankruptcy or potential bankruptcy
2. Heightened levels of anxiety
3. Depression
4. Traumatic experiences as a child or young adult."

When Justin shared these four with me in a conversation, my jaw dropped, as I realized I've experienced all four.

Rob and I can add a fifth to Justin's list: "addiction."

Addiction is doing something compulsively, in excess, that is not good for you: work, food, porn, drugs, alcohol, gambling, TV, social media, gaming, or shopping, to name a few. These addictions are soothing to driven entrepreneurs because they assist in numbing and distracting you from your internal pain and give you the dopamine hit you so desperately crave. It might sound crazy to say, but for a driven entrepreneur, building a multimillion-dollar company is soothing. They can get lost and numb themselves in the hustle and bustle of building the business. They never have to stop and look inside themselves, so they never think they are harboring any pain.

The solution is to understand and acknowledge the pain. Accepting it will speed up the process of eliminating it. Soon it will go away.

A 2015 study by Michael A. Freeman, clinical professor of psychiatry at the University of California, San Francisco School of Medicine, and an acknowledged expert on the mental health of entrepreneurs, found that 49 percent of entrepreneurs had dealt with some kind of mental health challenge: "People who are on the energetic, motivated and creative side are both more likely to be entrepreneurial and likely to have strong emotional states." He also noted that "different people have different strengths and different vulnerabilities. For people in business, if you're an executive or manager or founder, you need to understand yourself and manage yourself so you can play your strong cards and have strategies to manage your weaknesses."

Another 10 Discipline client, Mike Sullivan, president and CEO of Loomis, a full-service ad agency, lost half his revenue in ninety days. "It was terror," he shared. "Slashing my income, laying off people I loved, and finding the energy to hustle hard to rebuild my business was more than I was equipped to handle. I think many entrepreneurs believe they thrive on intense pressure and even wear it as a badge, but that's a grossly overrated orientation for me. At the time, my winning formula didn't include a lot of self-care. I learned the hard way that too much stress is brutal on the mind, body, and spirit. It was easily the most miserable time of my life. What's worse, I didn't have the scaffolding in place to catch my fall. And boy, did I fall.

"It started with sleepless nights and creeping anxiety that ultimately turned into gut-wrenching, all-consuming stress. So, I did what many self-respecting entrepreneurs do. I went to my doctor for a prescription. I got some clonazepam to calm myself down. I also tried a couple of prescriptions for sleep with varying degrees of effectiveness. I even got some Adderall to help with focus and energy so I could work extra hard and fast to rebuild my business. The side effects from the drugs made matters much worse. Before I knew it, I was swallowed up in a severe clinical depression. Then I made a suicide attempt. That earned me a compulsory week's stay in a hospital psychiatric unit, which, in retrospect, certainly beat the hell out of the alternative. It was a gigantic wake-up call. My business is not worth my life. Nothing was worth the awful toll my coping strategies took on my family. It was a very scary time for all of us.

"In the years since, I've shifted my thinking dramatically by incorporating many resources including a great therapist and no more medications. A decade later, my business has never been stronger, and, more importantly, I have never been healthier or happier. There have been setbacks in the years since then, as there always are, but my capacity for handling the ups and downs has grown by leaps and bounds."

This lack of peace in your life isn't necessary. Nor is the feeling of emptiness. You're simply trying to fill a hole that can't be filled with outer world "stuff."

Using The 10 Disciplines, we are going to show you how to fill that hole and experience a sense of wholeness. For now, the point of this Discovery is to help you become aware of what it means to be driven—the good, the bad, and the ugly.

The driven are the builders and the creators. They make a huge difference in the world. Rob and I believe that driven entrepreneurs have a direct impact on an average of about two hundred people in their lives (employees, vendors, customers, peers, family, friends, and acquaintances). You are already making an impact on these people, no question about it. But you have only scratched the surface of what is possible.

Just consider for a moment the idea that when you interact with employees, clients, family, and friends going forward, you could be more peaceful, joyful, loving, calm, creative, clear, sharp, connected, thoughtful, fun, and enjoyable. How might this affect them? How might they respond? What would that do for people's trust, comfort, productivity, and willingness to follow your lead?

One important closing point to understand about being driven is that our DNA makes it harder for the driven to do this inner work. The other 90 percent of the population find it hard, too, so imagine how much harder it is for us. But we know you are up for the challenge.

For now, though, there is nothing you need to do. Just be aware you are driven and understand the pros and cons. The how-to's are coming in part II of this book.

CHAPTER SUMMARY

The Point

You are driven. It is a blessing and a curse. You make a huge impact on the world but, unfortunately, you do damage to yourself and others. The damage is avoidable but repairable.

Three Practical Takeaways

1. Being driven is a gift. You are born with it. It is in your DNA. It is in your blood. Embrace it. Be grateful.
2. You may have pain (bankruptcy, anxiety, depression, trauma, and/or addiction). Acknowledge it and begin to understand your inner story.
3. There is an inner fuel coming that is much greater than the outer fuel you used to get here, which provides a tremendous sense of peace.

Before we move on, do you understand Discovery #1: I Am Driven? Do you get it? Please don't move on until you do. Reread this chapter if necessary.

It might help your understanding if you take a minute right now and make a personal list of your pros and cons of being a driven person.

Pros   Cons

_____   _____

_____   _____

_____   _____

Pros	Cons
_____	_____
_____	_____
_____	_____
_____	_____
_____	_____

DECISIONS ARE MADE OUT OF LOVE OR FEAR

This discovery was truly jaw dropping. It literally altered the course of my life. This seemingly simple idea goes very deep, opening all sorts of pathways. We want to prepare you: This chapter is quite lengthy. In fact, it is the longest chapter in the book because we will be taking you all the way to the root of fear-based decisions. If you stay with us, it may alter the course of your life as well.

Please consider the possibility that your decisions are made out of love or fear. It was so enlightening to realize this fact . . . and then, so painful to realize that *most* of my decisions in my life were made out of fear. Love means a decision is coming from your heart or True Self, and fear means it's coming from your mind or ego.

Love = Heart (True Self)
Fear = Mind (Ego)

The ego, often misunderstood as arrogance or other negative behavior, represents our conscious mind, self-identity, and the way we perceive ourselves. It helps us navigate the world and make decisions that protect and promote our well-being. It's an important part of who we are and is necessary for our survival. Our point is that ego is not a bad thing. But the ego can become overly dominant or rigid, and it's important for us to notice when this is happening, as it may cause us to resist change, hold on to past hurts, or push things away that threaten our self-perception. These are the circumstances that can cause us to make decisions from fear.

As you read on, you will see the lifelong battle of almost everyone on the planet. So often, when we human beings make a decision, feel an emotion, or have a thought, it is out of love (our True Self) or fear (our ego).

As a hard-charging entrepreneur, you are probably making ten times more decisions than the average person on the planet—who to hire, who to fire, who to meet with, how to invest in growth, what to sell, where to go on vacation, what to say to your spouse, how to handle an issue with a child, and so forth. Each time you make one of those decisions, it will come from love or fear.

Many of our clients believe that their fear has helped drive their success. Roderick Walker, founder and Visionary at Tavros, a twenty-four-hour residential agency that provides continuous care and services to adults with intellectual/developmental disabilities, realized that the fear that he wasn't good enough—or enough as a person—is what drove him for years.

Our hope is that you will understand, as you read this book, that fear is not a healthy motivator. One million years ago, our ego was vital. There was danger behind every tree and boulder. Our ego was protecting us from saber-toothed tigers! Today, we have complex lives with new versions of saber-toothed tigers, and we continue to make most of our decisions from fear. Our ego is still trying to protect us from harm.

Justin Maust, owner of Rackley Restoration, a property restoration company, fired his Integrator, a good friend, on a weekend because he feared his operations leader would leave if he didn't. As it turns out, the operations leader that he was trying to save ended up costing him more than $250,000 in losses because of negligence on the job. Justin said, "It's no wonder my Integrator and operations leader didn't get along!" Fear had clouded Justin's ability to see the truth of what was happening in his business.

Fear of Letting Go

Fear of loss, failure, or the unknown causes us to hang on to emotional attachments to business affairs, people, material possessions, and desired outcomes. We can become attached to our lifestyles and fear losing them. We can become attached to people and control them so they will not leave us. We can become attached to outcomes, such as becoming so focused on building our companies to a certain size that we lose sight of everything else and burn ourselves out—and, a lot of times, destroy our business and/or relationships along the way.

If you are experiencing any or all of these, you are not free. When you are attached, you are dependent on someone or something else for your happiness.

Psychiatrist and physician David R. Hawkins, in his book *Letting Go: The Pathway of Surrender*, describes these attachments as hooks. For example, when we have emotional or mental attachments to others, we have our hooks in them. These hooks can lead to control and manipulation.

Here is a challenging question. If you knew your significant other, best friend, or top employee would be better off without you, would you let them go? Could you take your hooks out of them? If you answered no, you are attached and are hanging on to them. You are making a fear-based decision. And obviously, this is not fair to them. In a healthy relationship, you choose each other. If that ever changes, it's okay—you should let each other go.

Let's look at the other side of that coin. Some people have their hooks in *you*. They will not want to let *you* go. If you would be better off without them, they should let you go. This scenario is the clearest way to understand fear- versus love-based decisions because personal relationships hit closest to home. All other fear-based decisions are typically less evident. Simply put, you should not be attached to anyone or anything, and no one or nothing should be attached to you. It is an indicator of fear.

You may have a large customer who is detrimental or abusive to your company, but you fear losing them because it may set back your growth plans and/or reduce profitability. They have their hooks in you (and you have your hooks in them). If you make your decision out of love, however, you will see clearly that you must let them go and trust that you will replace their business.

Your ego is incredibly crafty. It knows how to lead you to make fear-based decisions without you even realizing. For example, you are stewing about something your spouse did that upset you. You want to discuss it and clear the air, but you are suddenly afraid to. Your mind tells you that they will get upset. This brings up fears of losing them and being alone, or how you don't feel entirely worthy of your spouse. So you stuff it down to keep the peace and stay "safe," and you end up harboring resentment, which burns energy as it eats you up inside.

I remember learning in sales that "fear of loss is a greater motivator than an opportunity to gain," so you should sell the fear. We are wired to hold on tight to what we have, or avoid what we do not want, more often than we embrace the opportunity for growth and peace in our lives.

Advertisers know this well and prey on our fears. Their messaging includes such negatives as friends looking with disapproval at your lumpy gravy or the pretty woman who is disgusted if your teeth are yellow. News media does the same with their approach of, "If it bleeds, it leads." They suck people in with their daily reports about all the horrible events happening in the world. And politicians use fear-based tactics to get elected, misleading voters about the opposition. We have no one to blame but ourselves for falling for it, but it won't stop until we stop. When you reach a place of love instead of fear, you can cut through all the noise. The change starts with you.

These sales, advertising, and political examples show how our egos are running the show. Our ego has built a structure to protect us. The structure is a masterful way for our ego to head off any perceived pain. It thinks many steps ahead. But this ego structure is exhausting, drains our energy, and stops us from living free as our True Selves.

When I realized my ego structure for the first time, I was shocked, saddened, embarrassed, and disappointed. I felt like such a fraud. My Office CEO Ron Harrell's ego created a structure where he gave himself a role called "fireman." He would instruct his staff to give him the biggest issues the company was facing because solving the problem and being a hero made him feel good. Ron said it was one of the dumbest things he had ever done in his career. Being the savior and fixing everything was simply a way of feeding his ego, of feeling important and creating distractions so he didn't have to face himself. In addition, he was teaching his staff that when things got tough, they didn't really have to be accountable for their roles because he would take care of it.

The Self-Made Prison

If you are in pain, you fear judgment; you feel alone, or like you're never enough. How could you possibly listen to your heart? You are too busy building walls to protect yourself. Your ego thinks it's helping you, keeping you safe.

An entrepreneur shared a story with us about an outdoor birthday party when he was five years old. With almost his entire family present, the cake was brought out with lit candles and everyone sang "Happy Birthday." He froze. He could not blow out the candles, and they began to melt into the cake. Tears streamed down his face, and he ran into the house and hid under his bed. As it turned out, a family member was missing from the party. His father had been absent from his life. The boy had prayed for weeks that he would show up. From that day forward, his ego began protecting him by not allowing him to believe it was safe to love, that he must have done something wrong that made his father mad and he was not worthy of being loved. Not until he was forty years old did he realize that this yearning was controlling his entire life. He had built a wall around his heart to keep everyone out, including his True Self, and was making all of his decisions from fear, not love.

The sad reality is that anything that smacks of freedom to your ego gets turned into a saber-toothed tiger. For instance, let's pretend you decide it's time to free yourself up from running the day-to-day of your business, because you are so overwhelmed and not spending enough time doing what you love. So you have the thought to hire an Integrator to run the day-to-day of your company. All of a sudden your mind starts saying, "That's going to cost a lot of money. You will lose control of your business, your employees will think you are lazy, you will lose your identity, and you will be put out to pasture." As a result, you suck it up and spend the next five years with too much on your plate, unfulfilled and tired.

Your ego is not happy that you are reading this book right now. It does not want you to break free and shine. Your ego has you trapped in a prison, and what's crazy is, you don't try to break out. It reminds me of the line in the Kris Delmhorst song, "Everything Is Music": "Why do you stay in jail, when the door is wide open?"

This prison consists of the "protective layers" that we build around our True Selves, like the layers I created at age fifteen. Having all of those layers and trying to succeed in life is like running a race in a suit of armor. It's uncomfortable, heavy, painful, loud, and awkward. Shedding your layers would be like entering the same race in running shoes, a T-shirt, and shorts. Imagine how much more lightly, freer, and faster you would run.

These layers can fuse and harden over time until they resemble a block of marble wrapped around you. Yet it isn't real. It was created by your ego, and all that needs to happen is for you to chip away all the marble that isn't the real you.

It's time to remove all the unnecessary marble and reveal the masterpiece sculpture that is you—the real you, your True Self.

We're going to show you how to break free from your ego and shine. We'll take you four levels deep so you understand what has you trapped and can stop basing decisions on fear and start making more decisions from love. This way of making decisions will become your new fuel. You will find it to be a hundred times more powerful than the average person's fuel.

Here is The 3 Discoveries Model again. This time we urge you to focus on the four levels under Discovery #2. Starting at the top, "The True Self Level," you will go down through each as we share what causes fear-based decisions.

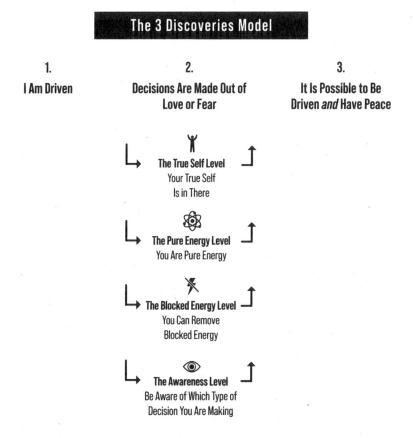

Those are the four levels of what causes fear-based decisions: first, the True Self level, followed by the Pure Energy level, then the Blocked Energy level, and then the final level, Awareness. We are going deep. If, at any time, it gets overwhelming or scary, just go back up to the main point of this discovery, "Decisions Are Made Out of Love or Fear," and reset. If you're ready, down we go.

The True Self Level: Your True Self Is in There

Your True Self is present at birth and remains within you throughout your life. It can become obscured quickly as factors from the world begin to influence our conscious self. These outside factors range from parents, friends, and teachers to the culture we grow up in and different life experiences. These forces change us and gradually push our True Self ever deeper inside us. Eventually, it is buried beneath a hardened "protective" shell. For many it remains buried in this prison for their entire life.

The concept of a True Self has many names—essence, spirit, innate self, authentic self, life force, or soul, to name a few. It's been studied by different cultures, spiritual gurus, philosophers, and religions throughout history. Because the True Self cannot be seen or measured, the science behind understanding it is limited. Some scientists and philosophers have attempted to explain it from a naturalistic perspective, regarding the mind, brain, and consciousness as potential components.

There are many ways to describe it. Merriam-Webster's Dictionary defines it as "an immaterial force within a human being, thought to give the body life, energy, and power." We prefer the term "True Self" and will use it throughout this book, but choose the term that resonates with you the most. The point is, you have a power source inside you, and it wants to be free. And when it's free, you make better decisions—and, therefore, have more energy, creativity, and impact.

Not until a few years ago could I finally, clearly see the structure that my ego had created. It was masterful. It thought twenty steps ahead. When anything was going to cause me pain, my ego knew how to head it off at the pass—through humor, redirection, creating a distraction, or the like. For instance, when I would meet bullies later in life, I could see them coming from a mile away. I'd start to feel a warning bell stir inside me from past bullying, and I quickly distracted them by telling a joke and redirecting their bullying behavior. As a result, I would have to be on guard and tense during the entire interaction. It was so exhausting.

Yet peace lies naturally within each of us. While working with clients, Rob will ask what peace feels like to them. Often, people have a difficult time describing it, but they usually use words such as "joy," "happiness," "self-love," and "ease." It is when they pause, and no longer try to describe it, that Rob knows they understand. Peace has a quiet tranquility and a serene state.

Peace comes as we free our True Selves.

Nathen Fox, CEO of Zen Fox Strategies, a business consulting company, shares that getting closer to his True Self has been a lifelong evolution of shedding layers. He had the longing to discover his True Self from early adulthood, which led him to try different ways to shed layers. Still on his journey, Nathen explains that as progress comes, "there is an opening and expansion, a freeing of myself." He describes the journey like surfing, "riding a wave down the face, then back to the crest where you hang on, and nature cooperates a little so you can ride down the face again. Each time you ride down the face, you are becoming one with the wave, eventually getting into the tube and having an even more exhilarating ride." For Nathen, life is more exhilarating as he sheds more layers.

At this level, all you have to do is begin to notice the structure your ego has built to protect you, and understand that your True Self is trapped in there and wants to be free.

As you become aware of the layers, I encourage you not to get discouraged. This is a beautiful discovery, the first step toward your awakening. Stay curious, stay kind, and stay present. When you try to shove your ego out of your way, it actually becomes stronger. Just relax and appreciate what your ego has been trying to do for you. You can also get help with this process. We will introduce you to a number of resources in this book and have provided a robust list in the "Resources for Shedding Layers" section in the back of this book.

Maggie, a friend and entrepreneur, learned to shed layers. Once she started to notice the layers, she knew that she was on the right path. Rather than the "effort and fight" she would normally call upon to come out on top, she began to realize her frustration and anger when things did not go the way she planned. When she finally let go, her business and personal life began to thrive. Her business tripled in size, and after years of trying, she became pregnant with twins.

We don't expect you to fully believe this concept—that the real you is stuck behind layers of your ego—yet. But what will happen as you implement The 10 Disciplines is that your ego will start to let go. The more you shine the light of awareness on it, the more its shield dissolves. For me, it was hard to believe at first. The best way I can describe the sensation that my True Self was present was when I briefly experienced no fear. A sense of calmness opened in the form of inspiration, clarity, confidence, and wisdom. During these moments, I would feel bursts of that calm. As I shed more, they kept coming, and I was being more and more me. I felt continually more love and less fear. My meditation practice greatly helped with this. And the bonus was being more connected with people, more creative in my work. I started making better, more productive decisions.

By shedding unneeded layers, you will shift from a scarcity-minded to abundance-based thinking. You will increasingly accept that your True Self will create endless opportunities you could not have imagined prior. Your True Self is loving, creative, confident, clear, intuitive, wise, and a bright ball of energy. You will realize this once you chip away all the marble. To help understand how to chip it all away, let's go down to the next level.

As we head down to the next level, if it's getting overwhelming or scary, go back up to the top, "Decisions Are Made Out of Love or Fear." You could also review The 3 Discoveries Model again, to help see the context.

The Pure Energy Level: You Are Pure Energy

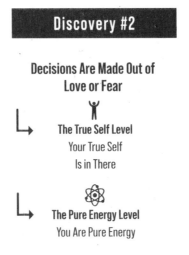

You may recall a time you met someone new and thought, "Wow, that person had great energy." Or maybe you reflected on how they had bad energy.

We are not talking about physical energy, such as your ability to run a marathon, or having endless energy while you are engaged in work. The type of energy we are talking about here is what we describe as your energy field.

Richard Feynman was a renowned American physicist who shared the 1965 Nobel Prize in Physics. He concluded that from the standpoint of quantum physics, all matter in the universe, including humans, is fundamentally composed of energy.

In his book *QED: The Strange Theory of Light and Matter*, he explains how the tiny objects that comprise matter exhibit properties of both particles and waves. This "wave–particle duality" and the inherent uncertainty in quantum mechanics led to the conclusion that particles such as electrons and photons go back and forth in a field. This leads to another conclusion: humans, who are made up of these same particles, can be viewed as "highly organized packets of energy."

Stephen Hawking was a globally renowned British physicist, cosmologist, and author. In his book, *The Universe in a Nutshell*, he writes about the fundamental principles of physics, such as the nature of space-time, quantum mechanics, and Einstein's well-known equation, $E = mc^2$, describing the relationship of energy and matter.

Hawking explains that humans, like all matter, are demonstrations of energy due to the mass–energy equivalence. Simply put, just like everything else in the world, humans are made up of energy because everything that has mass (weight) can be turned into energy, and vice versa.

You are a ball of energy. We are all balls of energy. It is scientifically proven. Some of us shine bright, some don't.

If this feels a little too woo-woo to you, you are not alone. I have been learning about how we are pure energy for almost three decades, and I still find it hard to understand.

David R. Hawkins, who has lectured widely at such places as Westminster Abbey, the Oxford Forum, the University of Notre Dame, and Harvard University, describes this energy as vibration. To illustrate it, he created a Map of Consciousness. Hawkins's map uses a logarithmic scale that ranges from 1 to 1000, which he calls the "Scale of Consciousness." It is derived from muscle testing (applied kinesiology), which Hawkins believes measures an individual's level of consciousness. The map is divided into tiers, each representing different emotional states and perceptions of reality. Lower levels include words like "shame," "guilt," and "grief," and higher levels include words like "love," "joy," and "enlightenment." People can vibrate very high or very low, depending on their state of consciousness. Or, said another way, they shine very bright or not at all. When you move up from fear-based emotions to love-based emotions, you shine brighter, and your energy is maximized. This high and low vibrational energy can also be described as positive and negative energy.

The energy we emit attracts a like energy to us. We are all connected by energy through exchanges that we cannot see. Maybe you have a friend who always seems to vibrate with high energy. When you are around this person, you also feel a positive energy within you rise. Or you may have a friend who vibrates with low energy that drags your energy down.

Which type of person are you? For many of you reading, I am guessing you would like to believe you are the former, the one who always seems to vibrate high. I hope you are. Because you are a driven entrepreneur, it's likely you do, sometimes. It's also likely that you vibrate low at other times and drain people's energy.

Remember the exercise you did in the opening of this book, when you removed everything from your life? Well, simply put, if you felt love and peace, you vibrate high. If you felt lonely and unsafe, you vibrate low. Wherever you are, it is showing up in a thousand different ways when you interact with people.

Dan Cornwell, a client and the managing director for Michigan at NFP, a provider of insurance, benefits, and wealth

Enlightenment	700+
Peace	600
Joy	540
Love	500
Reason	400
Acceptance	350
Willingness	310
Neutrality	250
Courage	200
Pride	175
Anger	150
Desire	125
Fear	100
Grief	75
Apathy	50
Guilt	30
Shame	20

solutions, struggled for years with people who had low energy and found himself drawn to people who vibrated with high energy. Not only that, he also would find that he was matching the energy of those around him. With this awareness, Dan began understanding the power of his own energy and his ability to raise the energy of those around him, and intentionally surrounded himself with people who vibrate at a higher level.

For example, people who are experiencing anger (vibrating low) tend to attract angry people. We've all heard the quote, "Misery loves company." These people typically make fear-based decisions. On the other hand, people who are joyful and at peace (vibrate high) tend to attract joyous, peaceful people. A psychological term for this is "emotional contagion," which is our tendency to mirror the mind states of others.

People who vibrate high literally repel people who vibrate low. It is unconscious. There are no words exchanged. It's just a feeling.

Here's the most exciting part. When someone vibrates low and does not shine bright, if they are surrounded by people who are shining bright with high energy, the brighter people will raise the vibration level of the people vibrating lower (assuming they are not repelled). Imagine that impact on the world!

Vibrating low is not something to be deeply concerned about. You are where you are, and it can vary throughout the day. Noticing when you are vibrating low will allow you to be mindful of the way you react and interact, as well as the way you feel inside. We will teach you in the next level how to remove blocked energy and shift to a higher vibration.

You have an intuition. This is your ability to tune into the field of energy created by our constant exchange of vibrations. We all have this intuition, but most don't use it. The good news is that once you vibrate higher and use it effectively, it gets stronger and your capacity to use it grows.

Now that you understand that you are a ball of energy, and that some people shine bright and some don't, the next step is to understand that when you don't shine bright, you have a block.

This block stems from a past pain or traumatic experience your ego is holding on to that is keeping you in a low vibrational state. It might be any of the real-life examples we've already shared: abandonment, sex abuse, bullying, rejection, betrayal, or humiliation. To shine bright, you need to remove the blockage. How? By dropping down one more level. That's where we are going next.

As we head down, again: if it's getting overwhelming or scary, go back up to the top, "Decisions Are Made Out of Love or Fear." You could also review The 3 Discoveries Model again to recall the context.

The Blocked Energy Level: You Can Remove Blocked Energy

Discovery #2

Decisions Are Made Out of
Love or Fear

↳ The True Self Level
Your True Self
Is in There

↳ The Pure Energy Level
You Are Pure Energy

↳ The Blocked Energy Level
You Can Remove
Blocked Energy

As Rumi, the thirteenth-century poet and theologian said, "Your task is not to seek for love, but merely to see and find all the barriers within yourself that you have built against it."

At some point from birth until now, it is likely that something negative or unpleasant happened that has stuck with you. You held on to it. Or like Rob and me, you might have experienced multiple jolts. It might have been a past wound, pain or trauma, shame, or regret. Whatever it was, our ego doesn't want it to happen ever again and buries it deep inside. So when some stimulus hits the block, it triggers our central nervous system and we try to understand our emotional reaction analytically. Unfortunately, this type of blockage cannot be dealt with through the mind.

For example, Mary grew up in a ranch-style redbrick home. She had a challenging upbringing filled with a great deal of trauma from verbally abusive parents. She got married and had two children. One day, while driving them to soccer practice, she passed a ranch-style redbrick home. A dark storm welled up inside her. One of her children asked an innocent question: "Mommy, can I have some more crackers?" Mary angrily lashed out at her child for asking for more food and told her she was a pig. Moments later, she wondered why she reacted so angrily and could not figure out why. She apologized to her child and handed over the crackers.

The trigger for Mary was seeing the ranch-style redbrick home. Simply seeing a home like the one she grew up in was enough to disturb her. Her energy was blocked by that trauma in the past and still affects her in the present.

In his book *The Untethered Soul*, Michael Singer calls the dynamic of your blocked energy causing a reaction "hitting your stuff." When this happens, he urges you to confront your negative thoughts and emotions directly, begin to let go of them, relax, stay open, process them, and move beyond them.

In the book *The Body Keeps the Score: Brain, Mind, and Body in the Healing of Trauma*, author and psychiatrist Bessel van der Kolk teaches us that past trauma remains in the body. He cites stories of people who don't remember their traumatic experiences at all because they bury them so deep, but the pain and the block still flare up. Some people do remember their trauma in vivid detail decades later, but it will stay buried until it is brought up and released.

Odds are, you have blocked energy. You may have been pushing it down for years. This is one of the reasons why people go to therapy, experience depression, or react adversely to circumstances in their lives.

Blocked energy stems from what has happened to us and actions we've taken toward others. Each of these situations leaves an imprint on our mental and emotional state. Unresolved issues like past mistakes, regrets, shame, and guilt often lead to mental unrest. In this level, you will learn ways to unblock this energy by forgiving yourself and others, letting the truth set you free, and ceasing to hold on. For now, let's focus on understanding what blocked energy means.

According to the Substance Abuse and Mental Health Services Administration, a division of the US Department of Health and Human Services, more than two-thirds of children report having experienced at least one traumatic event in their life by age sixteen. Examples they cite include:

- psychological, physical, or sexual abuse
- community or school violence
- witnessing or experiencing domestic violence
- commercial sexual exploitation
- sudden or violent loss of a loved one
- refugee or war experiences
- neglect
- serious accidents or life-threatening illness

In Rob's case, the trauma started at age eight with his parents' divorce. For me, it started at age six with sexual abuse. Are you aware of the past trauma you've had?

Growing up, real estate entrepreneur Brett Kaufman never felt like he was good enough. His low self-esteem stemmed from having had an abusive father who pushed him to be the best in sports, excel in school, always look good, and have proper manners. Perfectionism was a priority. This feeling that he was never enough emerged in his business life as he vigorously built his real estate empire with a perfectionist mindset. He would often be angry, argue intensely with contractors, and push hard for everything to be just so. Brett was afraid to fail and set on proving to his father that he wouldn't. While these blocks brought him many successes, he often felt unsatisfied with his work, which led him to not be fully present with his family.

In the article "5 Childhood Wounds That Could Still Be Affecting You," from *Exploring Your Mind*, a blog devoted to destigmatizing mental illness featuring content reviewed by mental health professionals, Lise Bourbeau, author of the book *Listen to Your Body, Your Best Friend on Earth*, lists these wounds and their effects:

1. Abandonment, which leads to fear of loneliness, fear of being rejected, and invisible barriers against physical contact.
2. Rejection, which leads to thoughts of being undesirable and worthless, and thus sparks more thoughts of rejection.
3. Humiliation, which leads to fear of disapproval and criticism, the destruction of self-esteem, and development of a dependent personality.
4. Betrayal, which leads to a tendency to mistrust and causes envy and negative feelings; often people experiencing it grow up to be controlling.
5. Injustice, which leads to feelings of ineffectiveness and uselessness, and develops into a perfectionist personality (i.e., a fanaticism for order and perfection).

Bourbeau adds, "Knowing and recognizing these five wounds of the soul that can affect our wellbeing, health, and capacity to develop as people, allows us to begin to heal them." Rob and I quickly realized that we suffered from multiple wounds on the list.

Please take a moment to think about any blocks you have or experiences that have caused blocks. I encourage you to write them down. Remember, blocks cause you to feel shame, guilt, sadness, trauma, pain, embarrassment, remorse, and/or anger.

_____

_____

_____

_____

_____

_____

At twenty-seven, Eric Rieger of WEBIT Services found out that his father was previously married and had two other kids. Sadly, Eric learned about his half-siblings when one of them, his half-sister, was murdered. For his entire life, even to his day, he feels betrayed that not only did his family hide this information from him, but they also robbed him of the chance to know his half-siblings. Eric still struggles with trust issues and blocks around this trauma, but with the inner work he is doing, every day gets a little better.

Michael McKinney, chairman of the board at AM Transport Services, which provides outsourced logistics services, didn't have one significant traumatic event in his past but rather a thousand paper cuts that have caused blocks in his life. His father grew up poor, in a dysfunctional home where he and his siblings were often left to fend for themselves. He was constantly concerned with what others thought of him and compensated by becoming successful at making money, buying things, and moving up in social status. In addition, it was important to Michael's father how he and his siblings looked and performed in school, who their friends were, and what others thought of them. He would constantly pick on Michael, transferring his fear of shame and inadequacy to him. This repeatedly damaged Michael's confidence, which led him to build structures to protect himself from being hurt, including always seeking approval from his father and others around him. "This is a block that I'm still working through. It has been very difficult to dismantle," he said. In business, Michael found that these blocks led him to question his decision-making, be indecisive at times, and look for consensus when strong leadership was needed.

When you remove the blocks and vibrate higher, you will attract even better friends and employees. The better the energy, the better company you attract.

Experts who study energy blocks use different terms to describe them: mental impressions, dense energies, recollections, or psychological imprints that make up our conditioning. In Sanskrit, they are called *samskāras—sam* (complete or joined together) and *kara* (action, cause, or doing). You can have fun with what to call them. I call them bricks or matzah balls. "Oh, this one is a brick in my chest," or, "Whoa, this one is a matzah ball." I have a friend who calls them hairballs.

Shedding Layers

For the last twenty-five years, I have been doing what many refer to as "shedding layers." I have taken steps and worked with people who helped me get a little closer to my True Self. For example, each year I travel to Boulder, Colorado, with two of my dear friends. The three of us engage a facilitator to help take us deep. During one experience, when the facilitator took me back to my childhood, something was triggered and I cried, hard, for a while. I'm still not completely sure what it was, but I released something that day, and I felt lighter immediately afterward. That's why I always say, when you shed a layer, there will be tears.

I also use talk therapy. I started in my twenties, but back then I was not ready to be honest with myself, so it didn't work that well. When you are honest, a process of unfolding happens. Each step unlocks another step. I started therapy again in my fifties after my awakening, and the process was profound.

The therapy took place over a very intense six months. My therapist had me create a list of all the pain, trauma, shame, guilt, and remorse I had experienced since I was born. I came up with over fifty memories! Some very minor, some major. We worked through every one. It was one of the more painful exercises I have ever done, but also incredibly therapeutic, freeing, and healing for me. I clearly saw how I had built my armor, and the unfolding subsequently freed me. I finally let go and forgave everyone and everything, including myself. I highly recommend this exercise, but only under the supervision of a trained professional.

Early on in therapy, I didn't fully understand what I was doing. It just felt good after each experience. I've now come to realize that these layers I shed were parts of the masterful structure my ego had created to protect me from ever feeling my pain from the past. I also didn't realize how strong my ego was, and how tight it was holding on. The work I did in the first twenty years chipped away at the structure a little. And then, in the last few years, it really came down. (To help you begin this process, Rob and I list resources, books, and experts in the Resources for Shedding Layers section in the back of this book.)

Curt Rager, Visionary at Autumn Insurance & Benefits, a provider of personal and commercial insurance and benefits, was left with a huge hole in his life when his mother killed herself when he was eleven. Healing from this trauma has been a profound struggle. Through faith, he found a way to forgive her and himself. He knew he needed to release the pain but found it difficult, as it was deep and residual. Curt spent time alone in the mountains working through questions and allowing his feelings to fully surface. He also spent time discussing his feelings of loss and pain with family and friends. Through prayer, talking, and crying, he was able to let her go. While doing the inner work, he realized that by forgiving his mother he also reinforced his connection to her. Curt came to the realization that he will always love his mother and can find peace in this love.

When you shed a layer and release your blocked energy, you shine brighter and you vibrate higher. That's why it is so important to understand in advance what you're trying to do. By doing this work, you will be freed from your pain and free to be your True Self.

The Process One Exercise

Here is a simple way to help you process a block that we call the "Process One" exercise.

Think of three past wounds, shames, or traumas. Write them down. Now, please pick the mildest and easiest one to process. This is very important: don't choose the toughest one.

Think of the one you picked. Now, take three deep breaths. Keep thinking of it. Feel your body. Do you notice any tension? Notice where in your body you are feeling the sensation. For example, you may notice tension in your stomach or chest. These are the most common places to feel blocks. Continue to focus on the sensation and where it is. Now, if that feeling were a shape, what shape would it be? If it were a color, what color would it be? Continue to focus on it, the location, the shape, and the color.

Now, sit with it and breathe. Focus on it until it's gone. Sometimes it's a minor sensation and it fades in less than a minute. Sometimes it's very painful and lasts for hours, even days. And you may cry a lot, which will pass. By starting with an easy trauma, you can experience processing a block and start to build the muscle.

If that exercise was emotional and you feel like you need some space, I encourage you to pause your reading and sit or take a quiet walk to allow your emotions to settle. If your emotions are extreme and you can't process them alone, please get help.

The goal is to see clearly what's actually going on and how you can shed all these layers. For some, the ones who are more willing to let go and surrender, this process will be quick. For others, this may take a long time. It depends on how hard your ego is hanging on. For me, it took a while. My ego was very strong and, as a result, I suffered for many years until I truly started to understand how to recognize blocked energy and to unblock it.

An episode of the TV sitcom *Modern Family* comically illustrates how much time it can take to unblock past traumas. The characters in the scene are a married couple, Mitchell and Cam. Mitchell has been going to therapy for ten years, dealing with traumas caused by his father while growing up. During a conversation with Cam, some issues Cam had with his own father come up, and Mitchell encourages him to seek out therapy as well. Feeling resistant, Cam skeptically sets up an appointment with Mitchell's therapist, and they attend the appointment together. When the therapist comes out to greet Cam and Mitchell in the waiting room, you notice how resistant Cam is to being there.

During this exchange, Cam begins sharing what happened to him and why therapy won't be helpful. By the end of his two-minute rant, he has fully processed all of his pain. He and the therapist never even sat down. The therapist then says, "That was extraordinary. I've never seen anything like that." She looks at Mitchell and says, "He doesn't need me." Of course, as Mitchell witnesses all of this, he is humorously dumbfounded, wondering why, after ten years, he still is dealing with his issues.

Again, the point is that people process blocks at very different rates. A select few will quickly and completely understand this concept, shed their blocks immediately, and be free. We hope you are one of them and that you believe this is possible. For the rest of us, the shedding will take a little (or a lot) longer.

Remember, each time you remove a block, you are chipping away a chunk of marble and revealing more of your True Self, vibrating higher, and shining brighter.

We have seen that people who vibrate lower tend to attract others that vibrate at a low level. For example, a person may repeatedly choose the wrong life partner, or, in business, choose the wrong business partners or employees. They keep attracting people with the same blocks, over and over, and they can't figure out why. The reason is they have not released a block and, as a result, must repeat the same patterns.

In *Letting Go*, David R. Hawkins shares a story about a woman who went through a traumatic divorce and was seeking psychotherapy. She was experiencing physical symptoms of a recurrent ulcer and migraine headaches. In addition, she had joined a group of mostly divorced women who were bitter, angry, and hated men.

The therapist suggested to her that she consider making one simple change for a period of three months before deciding to enter psychotherapy. Hawkins writes, "The recommendation was merely to discontinue her association with the group and with her bitter, divorced friends and instead, seek the company of people who had successfully reestablished relationships despite former divorces."

Realizing that "like goes to like," the woman accepted the challenge. The bitterness was getting her nowhere, and she was open to the idea that if bitterness attracts bitterness, then surely love can attract love. Hawkins concludes the story by writing, "In the company of happier people, she had an exhilarated awareness of how much negativity she was holding inside of herself . . . Her whole social life changed. She became smiling and happier. Her migraine headaches disappeared. Eventually, she fell in love again and joked that falling in love was the best cure she had ever discovered for an ulcer!"

This is a powerful example of how you can unblock energy. Simply change your circumstances and mindset. To do this, you must be open to new possibilities, like the woman in Hawkins's story. That account also shows how hanging on to blocked energy leads to adverse health effects. As has been said many times and ways, your block is eventually going to come up one way or the other, including as a physical disturbance or ailment, like my heart issue.

As we've shared, crying is a good way to unblock energy. Let it out. Remember, every time you shed a layer, there will be tears. Crying is cleansing. My hope for you is that you get to a point where you enjoy it. Crying is simply liquid emotion. I've seen far too many driven entrepreneurs hold back their tears for fear of looking weak or because of shame. It always saddens me when someone cries and covers their face. It's a sign that they are feeling shame. You were taught that crying is a sign of weakness, but it's not. It's powerful. It will help release your blocked energy. So cry it out. Try to cry and laugh at least once per day!

The same goes for anger—let it out. Doing this in a healthy manner can be a positive process. Anger is a human response that needs to be expressed appropriately instead of being suppressed. When you let your anger out, please do it in a constructive manner. Doing so can improve your state of mind, strengthen your relationships, and boost your health. Examples of healthy and appropriate ways to express anger are things like acknowledging it, not pushing it down, expressing it to the person or thing that is angering you, or deep breathing.

Being still is another way to bring up and unblock energy. One example is seated meditation. Author Anne Lamott has a wonderful saying about people's resistance to stillness: "My mind is like a bad neighborhood. I try never to go there alone." Most people can relate to this, as fear is a common reason why people have trouble with meditation. It's challenging to sit alone with our thoughts. But, as the Joseph Campbell saying goes, "The cave you fear to enter holds the treasure you seek."

When you sit in stillness, you create space. Blocks in your life begin to come up. During a stillness practice (more on this in Discipline #4: Be Still), you allow for those blocks to arise, be processed, and float away without judgment, like clouds in the sky.

There are thousands of ways to remove blocked energy. We've shared several in this level. We also will provide you with a robust list of resources to remove blocked energy in the back of this book.

You may also see an amazing surprise bonus benefit when you shed layers and remove blocked energy. As we shared in the first discovery, as a driven person, you likely suffer from addictions to numb your pain. Well, in our experience, when you shed layers, the desire for those addictions diminishes or completely goes away. You no longer feel the need to numb the pain, because there is no more pain to numb.

Before we drop down to the final level, it is important that you are following along. At this point, you should clearly understand that decisions are made out of love or fear, that your True

Self is buried beneath a structure your ego created, that you are pure energy that can shine brightly once all blocks are removed, and that you can remove all blocked energy.

As we head down to the final level, again: if it's getting overwhelming or scary, go back up to the top, "Decisions Are Made Out of Love or Fear." You could also review The 3 Discoveries Model again, to help see the context.

The Awareness Level: Be Aware of Which Type of Decision You Are Making

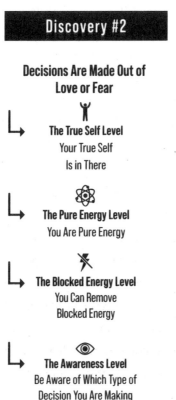

Discovery #2

Decisions Are Made Out of Love or Fear

The True Self Level
Your True Self
Is in There

The Pure Energy Level
You Are Pure Energy

The Blocked Energy Level
You Can Remove
Blocked Energy

The Awareness Level
Be Aware of Which Type of
Decision You Are Making

My dad, Floyd Wickman, used to share an analogy that describes awareness. When you buy a new car, let's say a red Chevy pickup, you drive off the dealer lot and head down the expressway. A funny thing happens: you start seeing a ton of red Chevy pickups. You think, wow, everyone purchased theirs today too . . . The truth is, you just weren't aware of them until you had one of your own.

Being aware is a practice of focusing on the present moment. Right here. Right now. Spiritual teacher Eckhart Tolle says, "With awareness comes transformation and freedom." Wellness author, PhD in molecular biology, and professor emeritus of medicine at the University of Massachusetts Medical School Jon Kabat-Zinn describes awareness as "the ability to pay attention to the present moment with a sense of openness, curiosity, and non-judgment."

At this final level, you are developing awareness. You start paying attention to situations, people, projects, and activities in your daily life. You will notice that some of these will feel positive and some negative. Every situation is different, whether it's work, family, friends, or places. In all of them you will become aware of when you are experiencing love or fear. Love is based in the heart and True Self; fear is based in your head and ego.

You can now go beyond just making decisions to a wider range of activities. You can recognize every love-based or fear-based feeling, emotion, thought, reaction, *and* decision.

Here are some examples that may help. While writing this book, which typically takes hundreds of hours of thinking, researching, actual writing, and editing, I shifted between love-based and fear-based thoughts, emotions, and decisions hundreds of times. At times I was so in the flow, coming from love and my True Self, that the words just poured out. At other times I would wake up at 2 AM in fear, asking myself, "Am I really going to share that? What will readers think?" Each time, though, I was able to clearly understand when it was my ego speaking or my True Self talking.

When I'm interacting with family and friends and I experience any kind of emotion, I'm aware of where it is coming from. When we are having a debate, for instance, sometimes the emotion will come from love and sometimes fear. The difference is so clear. The love-based debates are so much more enjoyable.

I've also come to realize that whenever a fear-based emotion comes up, most of the time I get a sensation in my stomach or my chest. When it's in my chest, I recognize it as relating to the past, and when it's in my stomach, it relates to the future. Another pattern I've noticed is that when I get a sensation in my throat, I'm holding back on saying what needs to be said. As you develop awareness of your emotions, please pay attention to where you feel them.

When Philip Pfeifer, a client and EOS Implementer (he helps entrepreneurs implement EOS in their businesses), finds himself feeling stressed, impatient, or aggravated, it opens up his innate curiosity. Often, he notices he is thinking about the past or the future and fearing that he will be hurt or that he is not good enough in some way. The sensations arise high up in his chest, and he feels like he can't breathe. Sometimes he notices them as high up as his throat, or that they are causing him to hunch while slouching his shoulders. By correcting his posture and loosening his cheeks and facial muscles, he begins to relax and return to the present moment.

Danielle L. Brooks, author of *The Extraordinary Ordinary You: A Manual for Self Discovery*, says a way to develop this skill is to "cultivate awareness." To assist in this, she created a tool called The Ego Interrupt. She explains, "The ego is not an evil aspect of who you think you are, it's just a compilation of ideas, beliefs, and perceptions that you thought was you. In fact, the ego is simply a faculty of the mind designed to bring you information, and it is your job as the discerner to accept or reject what information the mind brings you based on what feels true or right for you."

She explains that when you are aware of a thought or a feeling as it comes up, you can discern whether you are operating in ego or residing in presence as your True Self. If you are aware of ego activity, shine the light of awareness onto it and watch it disappear. It is cultivating awareness that interrupts ego activity. To determine whether you are residing in ego or True Self, she has created the following chart:

Ego Activity	True Self Activity
Fear	Unconditional Love
Dread	Safety
Uncertainty	Certainty
Anxiety	Inner Knowing

Ego Activity	True Self Activity
Anger	Intuition
Frustration	Calm
Stress	Ease
Difficulty	Peace
Guilt and Shame	Acceptance
Judgment	Freedom
Lack	Joy
Self-Doubt	I Choose
Worry	In Flow
Apathy	Open
Resignation	Wisdom
Cynicism	Oneness

Fear and anxiety led Jillian Lorenz of Barre Code Fitness to work while on vacation. She wanted to show her team that she places a priority on her personal life, but she still regularly found herself participating in work meetings while she was supposed to be relaxing. Her ego activity was her feeling of guilt for being away.

Let's say you have to decide whether to invest in a new product line in your business. Would your decision come from love or fear? If it is to diversify your product offering, the decision is from love. If it is to keep up with your competitors, because you think they know something you don't, it is probably from fear. Notice your emotions in the same way. Are the feelings love or fear? Maybe someone you thought was a friend in your industry poaches a longtime customer. Do you have a feeling of love or fear? If you understand that it's just business and you are competitors, that circumstances like these happen in business, you are coming from love and abundance. If you are angry and never want to speak with that person again because he stole something from you, you are coming from fear and scarcity.

Fear comes in many forms: stress, nervousness, tension, anxiety, and anger. To recognize them in your life, just start by being aware.

Over the years, I have worked with Daniel White, a guide who does what is known as energy clearing, a practice you can do with an expert to remove your negative energy. During one of my sessions with him, I shared how excited I was about a new business venture. I said, "It just feels so right. I can feel the excitement in my body." To my surprise, his response was that feeling was not necessarily good. In fact, what I should want is a feeling of knowingness. No sensation at all. The excitement was the dopamine hit that we, the driven, all crave. Knowingness is a sign that you are on the right path because you are not caught up in the emotion.

For driven entrepreneurs, that hit of dopamine is the external fuel. As we begin to free ourselves and make our decisions from love, we have better clarity and alignment with the circumstances that arise in our lives. We no longer look for the "adrenaline hit." We look for peace. We begin to just know it is right. The feeling is a combination of bliss, strength, and ease. The bonus is better decision-making.

This brings us back to awareness. Assuming you are now paying attention when you make your decisions from love (your

True Self), you will feel calm. If you are making them from fear (your ego), you will feel out of balance or disturbed inside.

At this level, we are asking you to be aware, when you make a decision or have a thought or emotion, of where it came from: love or fear.

Seeing the Veil

In *The Matrix*, the film's main character, Neo, is given a choice between taking a blue pill and a red pill. The blue pill represents the choice to remain in a familiar world where everything is predictable and controlled. The red pill represents the opportunity to awaken to the truth of his existence, even if that truth is difficult to confront. Neo chooses the red pill. After taking it, he clearly sees the Matrix, the prison he is in. This awareness sets him on a path to fight for freedom.

In a state of awareness/consciousness, we confront the challenging aspects of our lives. We all have them, and they can lead us to growth. As we grow, we gain wisdom.

This idea behind the Matrix has been known since the days of ancient India. In Hindu philosophy, *māyā* is the concept that all the perceptions we have in the world come from our biases, beliefs, and desires. It's all made up. It's also known as a veil, a barrier that gets in the way of the true nature of reality, which prevents us from seeing what's real, our True Selves, and the interconnectedness of all things.

This book is your opportunity to peek beyond that veil—to take the red pill.

If you think this is too heavy, let's dial it back to experiences you have every day. When you head to a meeting with a new client, what thoughts go through your head? They might run like this: What will they think? What if I fail? Will they laugh at me? Who am I to think I deserve a win? Will they accept me? Will I fit in? These are all from an outer, fear-based place, reflecting your worries about what the outside world thinks. If you go into that same meeting feeling light, clear, and at peace, operating from your intuition, knowingness, self-trust, and flow, you will be working from an inner, love-based place.

We call these two approaches inside/out decisions (emotions, thoughts) and outside/in decisions. An inside/out decision comes from your True Self, from within you. An outside/in decision comes from your ego and has to work through the many layers of the structure you have created to protect you from the outside world.

When you clearly understand these two approaches, you will see the distortion field your ego creates . . . also known as *māyā*, the veil, or the Matrix.

Once this context is clear, then you should clearly see the prison your ego has created for you.

A friend whom I will call Connie lived in Scottsdale, Arizona, for more than forty years, and she never thought she would leave, as her family and business were well established there. Connie and her husband had three kids between the ages of eight and fourteen. While having coffee with a friend, she mentioned that she and her husband had dreamed about moving to

Telluride, Colorado, to be closer to the mountains, hiking, and skiing. Her friend asked, "So why don't you move?"

This question stuck with Connie, and after sharing the idea with her husband, the two went *inside*, getting out of their heads and into their hearts. They realized what prevented them from making the move was fear of their family's reaction. The conclusion was a knowingness that this was the right thing to do. They moved within a year and are presently celebrating their fifth year there. Connie says that making this decision from the *inside out* was one of the best decisions she ever made.

Now, if you can consider the ego prison you are stuck in, you will clearly see all the excess marble that needs to be removed to expose your True Self—the masterpiece sculpture that is you. You will remove all of this marble in the second half of this book.

It's time to be free!

I understand that we are throwing a lot at you in this Discovery, and that we have gone very deep. To recap, let's reverse the levels and work from the bottom up to anchor your understanding and awareness of Discovery #2: Decisions Are Made Out of Love or Fear.

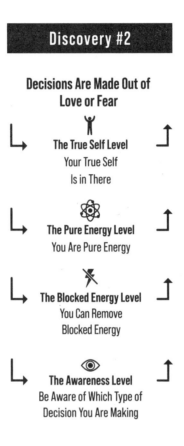

Discovery #2

Decisions Are Made Out of Love or Fear

The True Self Level
Your True Self
Is in There

The Pure Energy Level
You Are Pure Energy

The Blocked Energy Level
You Can Remove
Blocked Energy

The Awareness Level
Be Aware of Which Type of
Decision You Are Making

Starting from the bottom:

The Awareness Level: Be Aware of Which Type of Decision You Are Making. When you cultivate awareness, you begin to realize which type of decision (thought, emotion) you make: one out of love or out of fear. When you realize you are making a fear-based decision, work your way up the next level and go to the root of the block.

The Blocked Energy Level: You Can Remove Blocked Energy. At this level, you can remove the block that is causing the fear-based decision. This chips away the marble, and your energy will increase and shine brighter.

The Pure Energy Level: You Are Pure Energy. As you remove blocks, shine brighter, and vibrate higher, you reveal more of your True Self trapped behind the blocks and attract more of what you want in life.

The True Self Level: Your True Self Is in There. As you shine brighter, you start to see and feel your True Self, ultimately removing all blocks and reaching a point where your True Self is free and your decisions are love based.

If you begin making even just 10 percent more decisions from love than you are now, you are going to have a more fulfilling life. You will experience more growth, be more productive, have healthier relationships, and feel peace within. Even small steps are an improvement of great magnitude. You're playing the long game. Taking small bites. And making a huge impact in the long run.

We hope you now realize how straightforward this four-level process is. Not easy, but straightforward. You don't need to do anything right now; just be aware and understand that decisions are made out of love or fear, and realize what is at the root of a fear-based decision.

CHAPTER SUMMARY

The Point

Decisions are made out of love or fear. Love is a True Self–based decision, and fear is an ego-based decision. Fear-based decisions stem from a block that needs to be removed. When you remove the block and let go, your energy soars and you become more of your True Self. Be aware of which type of decisions you are making.

Three Practical Takeaways

1. Understand that your ego creates fear and a structure that causes you to hang on to emotional attachments to things, people, and outcomes in life, leading to decisions that are not best for you.

2. Become aware of your decisions and notice which ones are from love and which are from fear. Making even 10 percent more love-based decisions will have a huge impact.

3. Remove blocks and shed layers, and you will make more of your decisions from love—from the inside out—and you will be free.

Before we move on, do you understand Discovery #2: Decisions Are Made Out of Love or Fear? Please don't move on until you do. Reread this chapter if necessary. Reviewing The 3 Discoveries Model can also help your understanding. Once you understand, we can move on to Discovery #3: It Is Possible to Be Driven *and* Have Peace.

It might be helpful to take a few minutes right now and list the fear- and love-based emotions, thoughts, and decisions you've been experiencing lately.

Fear-Based   Love-Based

_____   _____

_____   _____

_____   _____

_____   _____

_____   _____

_____   _____

IT IS POSSIBLE TO BE DRIVEN
AND HAVE PEACE

Discovery #3 is my favorite. This is the epicenter of all our True Self content (The 10 Disciplines, The 3 Discoveries, every word in this book, our coaching, and all of our materials and resources). It all comes down to this. Rob and I are on a mission to show the world that it is possible to be driven *and* have peace while making a bigger impact. This discovery is the definition of being your True Self.

It took me twenty-five years to believe that drive and peace could coexist. I always thought you had to choose one or the other.

When I got my first taste of inner peace in my twenties, I was terrified. It happened immediately after each of my kids were born. I felt a level of peace that was incredible and indescribable. I'm quite certain it was love, which I'd never quite felt before. The feeling only lasted about an hour, because it scared the shit out of me. I'm pretty sure my ego pushed it away. One of my wounds that haunted me back then was never wanting to be a wimp, weak, or soft. I was a "tough guy," so peace felt like that to me back then. Because it conflicted with the persona I had created at fifteen, it was confusing. I thought that if I were truly peaceful, it would zap me of my drive. I would lose my edge, and then everything else, and all I would want to do is meditate in a hut on a mountaintop all day.

Turns out I was wrong, and I had to wait twenty-five years to understand that with peace, you can make an even bigger impact.

Peace is inherent within all of us already. You just have to remove everything that isn't you: fear, shame, regret, pain, and trauma. Here is the Rumi quote again, with a little twist: "Your task is not to seek for [*peace*], but merely to see and find all the barriers within yourself that you have built against it." You do not have to give up your drive. If you unite the two, you will be *more* successful, which we will illustrate in this chapter.

Upon this discovery, I would joke with people that someday I'm going to write a book called *How I Found My Soul and Kept My Business*. It was my way of saying, I really thought I was going to lose it all if I found peace.

Rob was similarly pinged with peace decades ago after reading *Wise Heart: A Guide to the Universal Teachings of Buddhist Psychology* by Jack Kornfield. While attending a silent retreat, he began to realize that his heart was at the center of his emotional and spiritual life, and it had the ability to cultivate love, compassion, forgiveness, and equanimity in life for a greater sense of well-being. The silence of the retreat allowed his mind to settle and understand the feeling of completely being in the present moment. By learning that, he cultivated an awareness and compassion for other people as well. He learned that this is a lifelong journey requiring discipline, patience, and practice. Last, he learned that it did not hinder his success; in fact, it provided more success, clarity, impact, and peace.

Here is one of the bonuses of Rob's discovery. He ran his business for thirty-one years. Thirteen years into it, as mentioned earlier, he sold it, but shortly after had an opportunity to buy it back. At that time he realized that being driven and having peace were both possible. Over time, he began to let go, feel the workings of his company more deeply, and bring his True Self to his work life.

The company culture began to flourish, as did the success and growth of the business. imageOne began working with *Fortune* 100 companies and, as mentioned, was named by *Forbes* as one of America's Small Giants, a list of companies that value greatness over growth, have sound business models, strong balance sheets, and steady profits, and are fixtures in their community. The peace that Rob was experiencing led him to the realization that if his company was going to make it to the next level and accomplish its ten-year vision, he was not the person to take them there (a love-based decision).

Rob's ego struggled with this for a while. He set out to find the perfect person to replace him, and over the next three years, he transitioned in his successor. He now sits in the owner's box with no formal role in the company but is able to devote his working time to the cause of bringing The 10 Disciplines to the world with me. His inner peace provided clarity to make that tough decision.

The True Self Model

The power of Discovery #3 is illustrated in the following True Self Model. It shows how the balance of using your drive to make an impact (working, creating, doing, serving) and experiencing peace (love, self-trust, being, presence) is your True Self.

Notice the words in each circle. In using the model, we find that different words resonate with different people. You get to choose your own. We love the words "impact" and "peace." That's what our driven selves want to do: make an impact and experience peace every day. One of our clients prefers "create" and "love" and uses those two words as her mantra. The point of the model is to understand that it is all about the balance of doing and being. Balancing the outer world and the inner world. For us driven entrepreneurs, it's about balancing our desire to work while experiencing calm. It's an incredible blend that enables us to be our True Selves.

You will notice words outside the model like "insecurity," "pain," and "trauma." These words are the barriers that prevent you from fully making an impact and having inner peace. These are the layers that you must shed.

Please choose the word that most resonates with you under Impact and the one that most resonates with you under Peace, as we have every client do. These can be your mantra. There is no bad answer, only the right answer for you. You can also use "impact" and "peace," use your own words not on this model, or even make some up, as some of our clients do.

THE TRUE SELF MODEL

BALANCE

IMPACT | **PEACE**

INSECURITY
FEAR
FAILURE
DOUBT
LACK OF CONFIDENCE

WORK
CREATE PRODUCE
CRAFT MANIFEST EARN
DO   VALUE   SERVE
DRIVE

SELF-TRUST
LOVE INTUITION BE
PRESENCE FLOW ENERGY
CONNECTED   LET GO
AWARENESS

FEAR
PAIN
TRAUMA
WOUNDING
EGO

OUTER WORLD   INNER WORLD

TRUE SELF
FREEDOM, CREATIVITY, & IMPACT
LET YOUR FREAK FLAG FLY
FLOWT

We hope that this True Self Model puts it all in perspective for you. Again, this is the epicenter of this work.

Flowt

Once you understand The 3 Discoveries and implement The 10 Disciplines, you will experience Flowt, the word we introduced to you earlier in the book.

Flowt happens when you learn to manage your drive, shed all that isn't you, and experience inner peace. When you do, you will be more creative and have more energy, your intuition will come online, you will be calm in the storm, you will have more ideas and think more clearly, time will slow down, you will be in your superpower, you will make better decisions, you will attract the right people, you will operate in the zone, you will experience an ease, you will develop a sixth sense, and you will unleash your wisdom.

Your blocks are deep rooted, but you can remove them. In the ten chapters that follow, you will find practical techniques that will loosen their hold. Then you'll discover what being driven and having peace can be.

You will be driven from the inside out.

You will replace the outside-in approach that used to give you ten times more fuel (competition, fear, pain) than the average person—the non-driven—with this inside-out approach (love, peace, intuition), which will give you *one hundred times* the fuel of the average person.

For example, our client Eric Rieger belongs to an industry group. The facilitator of the group encouraged Eric and his peers to run their businesses a particular way so they could set themselves up to sell in the advantageous private equity market. Although his instincts did not feel this was right, Eric found himself following the plan for fear he might miss out on a huge opportunity (outside in). One day, he wondered why he was ignoring the voice inside him, saying, "Whose dream am I living, anyway?" (inside out). With the guidance of his True Self, he decided that what felt most aligned for him was to sell a portion of his company to the employees by creating an ESOP (Employee Stock Ownership Plan). Eric's insecurities and lack of confidence went away. His ability to find peace allowed him to make a decision that aligned with his True Self while having the greatest impact.

Again, there is nothing to do at this point, other than be aware and understand that you can be driven *and* have peace. The fun begins in part II of this book. The 10 Disciplines provide the way.

CHAPTER SUMMARY

The Point

As a driven entrepreneur, you have the ability to be driven *and* have peace. You can have both. Gaining peace will not zap you of your drive or edge. Rather, it will increase your drive, and you will make a bigger impact.

Three Practical Takeaways

1. You do not need to give anything up to have peace. Peace is inherent within you already.
2. You will not lose your drive when you find peace. You will actually have more drive.
3. You can make a huge impact and have inner peace.

Before we move on, do you understand Discovery #3: It Is Possible to Be Driven *and* Have Peace? Please don't move on until you do. Reread this chapter if necessary.

Also, please don't move on until you understand all 3 Discoveries. Review the following 3 Discoveries Model to make sure you are fully aware of their power. Your understanding is vital because they are the outcome of implementing The 10 Disciplines for Maximizing Your Impact and Inner Peace in your life.

It might be helpful to take a few minutes right now and list all the ways you want to make an impact on the world around you, as well as all the ways that having peace will show up in your life.

Impact   Peace

_____   _____
_____   _____
_____   _____
_____   _____
_____   _____
_____   _____
_____   _____

The 3 Discoveries Model

1.   **2.**   **3.**

I Am Driven   **Decisions Are Made Out of   It Is Possible to Be
                          Love or Fear**   Driven *and* Have Peace**

The True Self Level
Your True Self
Is in There

The Pure Energy Level
You Are Pure Energy

The Blocked Energy Level
You Can Remove
Blocked Energy

The Awareness Level
Be Aware of Which Type of
Decision You Are Making

We have wrestled with the best way to illustrate The 3 Discoveries in a way that is understandable to everyone. We believe the model above is the clearest, but here is another way that one of our clients suggested we visualize it, which seems to resonate as well:

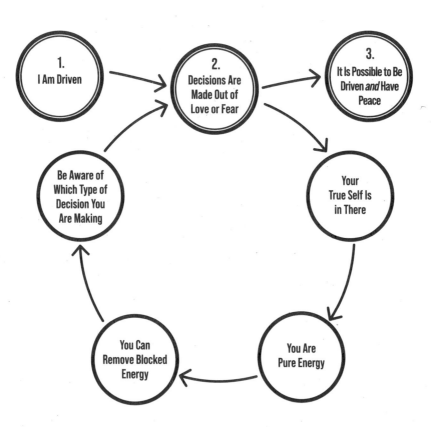

The 3 Discoveries Model

1. I Am Driven

2. Decisions Are Made Out of Love or Fear

3. It Is Possible to Be Driven *and* Have Peace

Be Aware of Which Type of Decision You Are Making

Your True Self Is in There

You Can Remove Blocked Energy

You Are Pure Energy

Now that you have discovered you are driven and know how that manifests in the world, and understand that decisions are made out of love or fear, you can shine bright, be your True Self, and make decisions out of love. Along with the discovery that you can be driven *and* have peace, the following are The 10 Disciplines to make all of these a reality for you. Let's get to work.

PART II

The 10 Disciplines for Maximizing Your Impact and Inner Peace

Now that you know *what* is possible (The 3 Discoveries), it's time to show you exactly *how* to do it (The 10 Disciplines).

For some, "discipline" can seem like a harsh word. We even considered choosing another. But as we received feedback from clients and test readers, we realized it is perfect. "Discipline" does not have to mean rules, regulations, restrictions, punishment, or something you do to others. In our sense, it means intentionally applying standards to achieve meaningful objectives (freeing your True Self).

The 10 Disciplines are designed to maximize the impact and inner peace of a driven entrepreneur. They are incredibly simple. But please don't let that fool you, because they are also very powerful. They will greatly increase the impact you want to have on the world by helping you fully tap into your driven DNA and bring to the surface all of your skills, abilities, and gifts.

They will give you tremendous peace by creating a foundation to open space in your mind; granting you time to do the inner work and shed everything that isn't you; freeing you from your ego; and giving you a sense of joy, fulfilment, clarity, and presence.

Simply put, they will help you become your True Self.

As we mentioned earlier, The 10 Disciplines have evolved in talks, books, and videos since their unveiling five years ago. They have transformed from being focused entirely on your outer world success by helping you become more productive, energized, efficient, effective, and impactful. They still will very strongly influence your outer world, but we've now learned that they also have a tremendous impact on your inner world success. They help you reveal the real you, chip away anything that isn't you, and aid in making more and more of your decisions from love and not fear, enabling you to feel and be free.

With that incredible combination of helping people master their outer and inner worlds, they are having a massive impact on driven entrepreneurs' lives.

We're excited to present the expanded and improved version of The 10 Disciplines and invite you on this journey with us. When you use them to free your True Self, your creativity will spark in a way you never knew was possible. This spark will lead to more and better ideas regarding the impact you are here to make on this earth.

When you incorporate the Disciplines into your life, you will notice a positive shift in your energy. You will be vibrating higher, more regularly, because you will have clarity, boundaries, and peace. Time will slow down.

To receive maximum benefit from the Disciplines, please commit to incorporating all of them into your life. Each one stands on its own, but together they have a synergistic effect that magnifies their impact, which will give you an exponential return.

In each chapter, you will receive how-to's for mastering each Discipline and three practical steps to reflect on. We encourage you to have something to write with as you read.

It is now time to shed all the layers, remove all the marble blocking your True Self, and reveal how you can truly change your world.

Let's begin.

10-YEAR THINKING

We will begin each chapter with an italicized statement that is the main point of the Discipline. If you apply the statement to your life the way it is written, you will get maximum benefit. The statement for this Discipline is:

Shift your mind from short-term thinking
to thinking in ten-year time frames.

This first Discipline will literally transform your life. It transformed mine.

If you're like most driven entrepreneurs, you are preoccupied with today, this week, this month, and maybe this year at the most. You want it now. Yet this short-sightedness is limiting you.

When you shift to long-range thinking, time will slow down. A feeling of peace will come over you. You will start to make better decisions. You will become more consistent. And the irony is that you will get to where you want to go faster.

I was thirty-five years old when I shifted to this mindset. I'm convinced I have accomplished more as a result. As the saying goes, "People *overestimate* what they can accomplish in a year, but *underestimate* what they can accomplish in ten years." The reality is that you can accomplish anything in ten years. As motivational speaker Les Brown once said, "All you need is a good decade."

For some people, thinking in ten-year time frames is challenging. Many can't think past today. If that is you, I encourage you to shift your mindset. If you really struggle with this Discipline, try aiming for this year, possibly three years into the future, maybe even five for starters. Whatever you feel ready for. Just know the intention is to eventually get to ten years.

Regardless of where you are now, please pause for a moment and follow this three-step exercise:

Step 1. Write the exact date ten years from now.

Step 2. Write the age you will be on that date.

Step 3. Take yourself there mentally, ten years from now at that age. Write down the number-one most important goal that you will want to have accomplished by that date. (You can write additional goals that come to mind as well.)

_____

_____

_____

_____

_____

What you write might have to do with the income you will generate or your net worth. You might foresee a major milestone for your company. You might want to improve your physical health. You might want to change a personal relationship. You might choose to fully become your True Self. There is no wrong answer. Yet for this Discipline to be productive right now, you must write down a long-term target to get your neurons firing.

When Lynn Rousseau of The Conscious Leader first learned of 10-Year Thinking during our program, she thought, "I'm not sure about this. I'll be seventy-one!" During the 10-Year Thinking exercise that we teach, she was inspired to establish a Coaching Academy. Using 10-Year Thinking shifted the way she thought about her business, and today she makes decisions about how to collect and organize the company's intellectual property with the future academy in mind. She also thinks differently about how to organize and structure training for their coaches so that everything they are doing is building the foundation of the academy.

Next, think about everything you have going on right now. All of your goals, plans, activities, and calendared items, and your current to-do list. Examine each one in light of what you wrote down. Do they all align with that 10-Year Thinking? If not, you have some course correcting to do.

For example, when I was creating EOS, I decided that I wanted to have ten thousand companies running on EOS within the next two decades. When I set that goal, I had only fifty companies. I had no idea how to get the rest. But the EOS Worldwide leadership team spent two full decades making ten-year decisions, and I'm happy to say that we achieved it, almost to the day.

My business mentor, Sam Cupp, taught me what he called the "ten-year business cycle." He said, "Every ten years you're going to have two great years, six good years, and two terrible years that can put you out of business." His advice has held up since he shared it with me more than thirty years ago.

Whether a downturn is caused by a pandemic, terrorist attack, recession or depression, war, or general business ups and downs, that ten-year cycle lets you know it's coming. You can count on the unexpected every ten years for the rest of your life. The point is, don't be surprised by it. Operating with a ten-year horizon will keep you steadier and making better decisions through the tough times.

The 2000–2001 dot-com crash and the Great Recession of 2008–2009 were blips in the grand scheme, although most of us with businesses didn't feel that way while going through them. At the time, it was brutal. Yet how often do you think about either of them today?

During every ten-year cycle, you will ride ups and downs. If you are always focused on the here and now, you will lose sight of the big picture during the turbulence. You will get caught up in the current growth spurt, downturn, or crisis. By taking a ten-year view, you will see, in the grand scheme of things, that a downturn is merely a flash in the pan.

The first company Rob started, imageOne, was one of my first clients to run on EOS. He learned early on about the ten-year business cycle. The understanding has served the company well over the three decades they have been in business, but never more so than in March 2020, the beginning of the

COVID pandemic. As the world shut down, Rob recalls looking out the window of his downtown Detroit apartment at the
beginning of a March workday and seeing empty streets. They
were usually bustling with people grabbing their coffees and
heading into the many office buildings in the area. imageOne
provides managed print services and multifunction/copier sales
to companies throughout the United States. Rob thought, "If
this lasts a long time, we could be in big trouble." If people
stopped working in offices, they would not be printing as much
and wouldn't be purchasing imageOne's products. It could even
put them out of business.

As the pandemic continued and working from home became
widely accepted, the CEO running imageOne, Josh Britton, was
grateful they had prepared for the worst. The entire team is composed of ten-year thinkers, so they were able to see and understand what the long-term outcome was and what they needed to
accomplish. They also had a strong balance sheet with cash in
the bank and access to more in order to sustain operations for
an extended period if needed. Thankfully, they made it through
and have become a stronger company as a result.

The point of the ten-year business cycle is to be prepared.
Knowing that the two tough years out of ten are going to come,
the first way to prepare is that you must have cash reserves.
Always have a minimum of six months' operating expenses in
cash sitting in a personal and a business account so you and your
company can endure at least six months of not bringing in any
income. The second way to prepare is to know and accept that
it is coming. Then, when it hits, you'll just say, "Here it is," and

get to work. I was thrilled to hear from so many people who told me, because they had adopted this discipline, they were prepared when the pandemic hit.

10-Year Thinking is about more than goal setting, although you should still have short-term goals. You're reprogramming your brain to think in a longer time frame. You'll make better short-term decisions, and you will get to your goals faster.

Josh Holtzman experienced the amazing benefits of 10-Year Thinking when he owned and ran American Data Company, an IT services firm. At a time when his company was generating $4 million in annual revenue, he set his eye on making it a $40 million company in ten years. Yet when he set this target, he and his leadership team had no idea how they were going to reach it. But once they committed, the answers came. Making ten-year decisions, the company joined forces with another player in their space. Unfortunately, they realized a few leadership team members weren't on board, so they replaced them with people who had greater experience and unflinching commitment. They hit $40 million right at the ten-year mark.

This Discipline also improves your presence in the here and now. In my many years working with driven entrepreneurs, I have witnessed firsthand how quickly they can get distracted. They love having multiple balls in the air and looking for the next greatest opportunity. These distractions aren't all bad. Creative thinking and an open mind lead to breakthroughs. 10-Year Thinking will help you decide where you should place your creative attention. It can bring us back to what matters most. For instance, if you run a company that excels at manufacturing widgets, and all of your 10-Year Thinking is focused on being the most respected, highest-quality widget manufacturer, it's pretty clear that, although you love working out every day, you probably shouldn't purchase a gym franchise.

10-Year Thinking will help free you because you'll stop worrying about the short-term small stuff. You'll stop doing things that don't align with what you see in ten years. It will also increase your energy, impact, and peace because you'll have a long-range vision to motivate and guide you.

Long-range thinking begins the shift from fear-based decisions to love-based decisions. It helps calm your mind, ego, and central nervous system. You can then start to see what you truly want, from the inside out, which then drives your actions and decisions in the here and now.

It's the same as why you brush your teeth. Brushing is a small daily action that moves you to a long-term outcome of having healthy teeth and gums and a better chance of living a longer life.

Creating a 10-Year Vision

If you want to build on this discipline, you can also create a 10-Year Thinking Vision or do a visualization exercise.

A 10-Year Thinking Vision can be a written story that paints a vivid picture of what your future looks like. It can also be a bullet-point list or one to two sentences. When writing your story, always use the perspective that the goal of your vision has already happened or is happening at this moment. For example, if your 10-Year Thinking Vision is to take a trip to Africa, you would write, "My trip to Africa was enriching and changed my view on the world. I will never forget our five days on safari—seeing the animals up close and being able to photograph them was amazing. As I look across my office at the pictures I had framed and hung on the wall, I remember the experience and smile."

Here is a five-step process to create your 10-Year Thinking Vision:

Step 1. *Pick your time frame.* Go ten years out. Write down the date.

Step 2. *Reflect for a moment on your accomplishments.* This is an exercise to get your mind working and in a positive mindset. It will also remind you what you are capable of. Write a list of accomplishments you've had in your life. After each, write one or two words about how it made you feel. Try to focus on *your* accomplishments versus those of others. For example, if you have children, their accomplishments are theirs, not yours.

Step 3: *Write the first draft of your 10-Year Thinking Vision.* The first time through is only a draft. Let it flow. Try to keep the writing going without much critical thinking—you can edit it later. Feel free to make bullets or write a story. Go big. We urge you to consider adding becoming your True Self, the impact you want to have, and what peace might feel like.

This is an opportunity to start bringing this work to life. Don't let fear get in the way. Write from love. Tap into your heart. What would be possible if you had no fear? Include all aspects of your life, personal and professional.

Step 4: *Share it with your significant other or business partner if you have one.* Once you have completed the first draft, we encourage you to share it with the people along for your journey. For example, if you have a significant other or a business partner, you should be in alignment. Our clients find this to be one of the most rewarding aspects of the 10-Year Thinking work. It can create a stronger bond with the people around you. Being on the same page together brings a wonderful sense of clarity, feeding into the love-based decisions you make today. It's so powerful to create a 10-Year Thinking Vision together.

Step 5: *Write your final draft.* Clean it up. Polish it into one sentence, bullet points, or a vivid story. Whatever works best for you.

Now that you have a strong final draft in place, our hope is that you will begin to cement it in your mind. You'll derive incredible value from reading your 10-Year Thinking Vision regularly. Remember, it is not goal setting. You're creating a mindset that directs your daily actions in the present moment and will lead to great shorter-term goal setting.

In addition, I have a habit I call "Seeing It Every Night." When I set the twenty-year goal of ten thousand companies running on EOS, I saw it every night when my head hit the pillow. I do this with all of my big goals. I urge you to do the same.

During an interview I did with Rob for the audio version of my book *The EOS Life*, he asked me if I could ever have imagined the success that EOS Worldwide has experienced. My answer? "I saw it every night."

In the book *You²: A High-Velocity Formula for Multiplying Your Personal Effectiveness in Quantum Leaps* by Price Pritchett, he explains the power of long-term thinking this way: "You must focus on ends, rather than means." He explains, "You must rivet your attention on that spot where you are to land. Once you do that, it's almost as if you magnetize yourself to the ways and means involved in the methodology for getting there. Solutions begin to appear. Answers come to you."

In Robert K. Cooper's book *Get Out of Your Own Way: The 5 Keys to Surpassing Everyone's Expectations*, he shares a quote from a Tibetan archer. For centuries these archers have had a reputation of being among the most accurate in the world. The archer states, "I saw the target. Then I simply sent my strongest line of energy toward it." Cooper goes on: "The arrow of life always follows the strongest line of energy. It goes where you commit every fiber, every molecule of your being . . . what matters are commitments of being. Those commitments form the unseen channels that guide you toward the results you desire."

Or, in the words of Yogi Berra: "If you don't know where you are going, you might not get there."

10-Year Thinking, along with using visioning and visualization, can prove to be powerful.

Going Beyond Ten Years

This Discipline is all about changing from short-term thinking to thinking in long-range time frames, to shift your mindset and energy. Once you let go of short-term thinking, your mind will be free and you will have a better, more peaceful quality of life.

"Long term" is a relative term. We want you thinking *at least* ten years into the future. The reality is that we'd love you to think in twenty-five-year, even hundred-year time frames. Dan Sullivan, the number-one entrepreneur coach in the world, teaches twenty-five-year thinking in his Strategic Coach Program. I created EOS to last at least a hundred years. Whether it does or not, I can't control the outcome. But creating it with a hundred-year time frame in mind led to better decisions while I was creating and growing it, and so far it has lasted and expanded rapidly for more than twenty years.

Ultimately, the Discipline is actually about setting forth your intentions, putting out that vibration to attract everything to you, and doing the actions daily that align with making your vision a reality. For instance, you might see yourself far into the future happily married, as your True Self, with a $100 million company that makes a huge impact. If that's true, then today's actions should reflect those intentions.

Whatever the time frame, your actions and shorter-range goals will become more intentional toward that end than ever before. According to Anese Cavanaugh, author of the book *Contagious Culture: Show Up, Set the Tone, and Intentionally Create an Organization That Thrives*, being intentional means "consciously choosing how you show up, engage, and interact with others in every situation. When you are clear about your thinking, that is exactly what happens."

With that as a jumping-off point, please consider the idea that there is no time. Only the present moment exists, the past is over, and the future hasn't happened yet. As you learned, the past holds on to us through blocked energy, and our ego likes to believe it can control the future. These obstacles make life challenging. You might consider the idea that these are mental/ego constructs and not reality. After all, if we are in the present moment, those things are not happening.

CHAPTER SUMMARY

The Point

Shift your mind from short-term thinking to thinking in ten-year time frames.

Three Thought Prompts

1. Write down an action you took in the last week that *does not* align with your 10-Year Thinking.
2. Write down an action you took in the last week that *does* align with your 10-Year Thinking.
3. Write down one thing you will change in your life to align with your 10-Year Thinking.

_____

_____

_____

_____

_____

_____

_____

_____

_____

_____

TAKE TIME OFF

Here is the main point of this Discipline:

*Take 130 days off per year and don't
think about work the entire day.*

Like most of the Disciplines, this one is easily understood but not easily executed.

Here are a few of the activities that clients proudly share with us when they return from vacation. "I cleared out all of my emails!" "I read the latest business book!" "I finally caught up on all the industry and business news!"

That's not a vacation. That's not time off.

We intuitively know we should take time off from our work lives, but in our connected world, it rarely happens. You can't go, go, go all the time. You have to turn your brain off. As Stephen Covey said, "You have to 'sharpen the saw.'" Put another way, you have to stop and refill your tank.

Recently, Rob was having a conversation with a driven entrepreneur. She eagerly shared with him that she had not taken a vacation in more than three years, saying, "I love my work, and there is nothing else I would rather be doing."

She is not the only person we've heard that from over the years, only to later hear how they went so hard that they burned themselves out. Maybe you are the unicorn in this world who works all the time, has no hobbies or outside interests, *and* has people in your life who love you, don't mind that you aren't spending time with them, or that when you do, you aren't fully present. We have yet to meet that unicorn.

You must work hard *and* play hard. Unplug from work, turn your brain off, and recharge your batteries.

I take 150 days off per year, which includes a sabbatical for the entire month of August. I've done it for more than twenty years, and I'm convinced I'm further ahead because of it. When I return from time off, I get more done, have more energy, and have more creative ideas that make an impact. And now that I've "shed many layers," I am much more present with my loved ones when I take time off, which has led to much better relationships.

I've been able to do all of that *because* I take time off. You have to allow time away from work in order to create clarity and space to do the work.

Plus, when you unplug and then come back to the business, you view problems differently . . . more clearly, almost from an outside perspective. As the old adage teaches us, "When I go slow, I go fast."

You can't have your foot on the accelerator all the time and expect to shed layers and find peace. If you are going nonstop, you are hiding behind your work. You are numbing your pain.

Entrepreneurs often push back by saying, "I can't take time off," "I don't like to take time off," or "That's not how I work." Some people just don't know how to turn it off. They're incapable of taking a break. They need to work. They feel like they're supposed to be working.

Please understand that is a disorder. Remember, most driven people have a work addiction—they are workaholics. They are numbing themselves with busyness.

When you take your foot off the gas pedal, the healing begins.

It's like the necessary one to two hours of deep sleep we need each night—the most restorative stage—when your brain waves, heartbeat, and breathing slow down. Your blood pressure drops and your muscles relax. This stage of sleep improves memory and learning and produces growth hormones. Your energy is restored, your cells are regenerated, and your immune system is strengthened. All because you stopped and slept.

Imagine if you didn't get enough deep sleep. It's the same as working all the time. You deprive yourself of the many benefits going on under the surface that you can't see. Stopping starts the healing process and creates the opening for the subconscious ideas bubbling inside you to come to light.

One of our clients was a workaholic, and as she made her way through The 10 Disciplines, she began to realize it. Awareness is the first step. As she worked on this Discipline, she boldly committed to taking two extended vacations and not thinking about work the entire time. Both entailed traveling: a ten-day trip to Costa Rica and a three-week stay in India.

While in Costa Rica, she noticed that after three days she began to feel extremely uncomfortable. After the excitement of arriving and getting settled had passed, she didn't know what to do. She tried to get into a routine but felt the pull to check her email, read a business book, or even call the office. Thankfully, she did not do any of those things. We should note that she did let her team know prior to the trip that she would not be checking email or calling in—she would be completely unavailable. Being a driven entrepreneur, she did not want to fail at her personal challenge to turn it all off.

The discomfort she was experiencing was a form of work–life detox. It lasted two more days, and then she began to hit her stride. As her mind and body began to settle, she started seeing the world more vividly—the sights, smells, tastes, and sensations of an exotic land. She realized that the uncomfortable feeling was opening up space for her to work on her inner world: freeing her mind, unshackling herself from her ego, and bringing her closer to her True Self.

For some, taking time off can seem unproductive. They feel that not being at work is the perfect time to catch up and think about work. Yet that is just another form of everyday work clutter. Committing to taking time off and not thinking about work opens up space in your mind and body. With this space, you will have the freedom to do the inner world work—the most rewarding work you will do.

Imagine a time in your life when you had a clear mind and a rejuvenated body. This feeling is available to you whenever you want. Taking breaks will help you begin to Flowt when you get back to work. You will be more productive, creative, rested, clear, and impactful.

A client of ours, Denver Nguyen, the CEO of Wayfynder, which provides corporate coaching, took two weeks off without thinking about work the entire time. He shared, jokingly, that it was very hard, comparing it to meditation but expanded for two weeks.

Denver's time off provided him the space for his mind to roam, which sparked his creativity. As he became more in tune, he wondered, "What does my soul want to express? What is my unique creation?" The time away provided him with the clarity to change the vision for the company. Its vision originally was to "democratize access to coaching to all levels." This vacation led him to implement a new and inspiring vision: to "make self-actualization at work commonplace"—that is, Wayfynder wants to teach the working world that they can bring their True Selves to the workplace.

Once you are committed to not thinking about work, you can begin to determine how you will use that time. The choice is different for all of us. For example, I like spending time with my wife, kids, and friends, traveling, reading, bike riding, walking, going to see movies, and relaxing. Rob enjoys hiking, hanging out with his wife, watching college football and professional tennis, and traveling with his family.

Make a list of your passions and interests. Examples are hiking, golfing, painting, playing an instrument, doing deep personal work, reading (non-business) books, bird watching, traveling, hunting, helping out in the community, hanging out with friends and family, moviegoing, bike riding, going for walks, whittling, gardening . . . the list could go on for pages!

What Is Your Magic Number?

The process starts when you decide the number of days off you will take per year. Commit to that figure in writing. We recommend at least 130. If that sounds like a lot, here's the math. If you're taking every weekend off, you're already taking 104 days off. Now add in your holidays and vacations, and you'll reach that number. As you do this exercise, commit to not thinking about work on any of these days off. This includes, as mentioned, not checking email, reading business books, catching up on business and industry news, or making a quick call to "check in" with the office.

To determine your days off, bring up your calendar and go through every day, week, and month from today's date through the next twelve months. Starting with the goal of 130 days off annually, block off on your calendar the Saturdays and Sundays that you will not work. If you block them all, that's 104 days. Next, block off all holidays that you will be off, followed by any vacations you have scheduled. Add up all the days that you blocked off, and you have your baseline. Now, build from there and try to get to 130 days over the next twelve months. If 130 days aren't possible, use what you come up with as your baseline and build on it each year.

Here's a tip when taking vacations: block an entire day before and after each one. I call this "cushioning your vacations." These are not days off but a day to prepare for your upcoming absence and a day to catch up after you return. This will make for a much more relaxing time off and greatly reduce your stress when leaving for, and returning from, vacations.

We encourage you to include significant others (spouse, business partner, management team) in your life in the Take Time Off Discipline. Set up a time together and go through the same process of looking at each other's calendars so you are on the same page with the time you will be off and not thinking about work.

As an additional challenge, we encourage you to schedule a one-month sabbatical. You have likely worked long and hard to get to this point in your life. You've earned it. As I mentioned, I have taken the month of August off every year for more than twenty years. I'm convinced it has greatly increased my energy, creativity, impact, and peace. I always choose one "shedding" experience every sabbatical.

If you haven't taken a sabbatical, it will require some preparation. Make sure you share your intentions with your significant other and the business stakeholders in your life. We also recommend you do a test run by taking a week off a few months prior to your scheduled sabbatical to stress-test and determine what systems and backups you need to tighten up or improve. By doing this, you will have a peaceful sabbatical and not think about work the entire time.

If we haven't convinced you of the value of taking time off, here's one last attempt.

Time off allows for your mind and body to stop and let everything in life catch up. It creates the space you need if you want to make a bigger impact and have inner peace. If you struggle with time off, face the discomfort you feel. You were not created so that you can work 24/7/365. Go to the root of the fear and process it as you learned in Discovery #2, Decisions Are Made Out of Love or Fear.

CHAPTER SUMMARY

The Point

Take 130 days off per year and don't think about work the entire day.

Three Thought Prompts

1. Does your time off align with your 10-Year Thinking Vision?
2. What will be the most challenging part of taking time off and not thinking about work the entire time? What can you do about it?
3. To what extent does your work shape your identity?

_____

_____

_____

_____

_____

_____

_____

_____

_____

_____

_____

KNOW THYSELF

The main point is to:

Be your True Self 100% of the time, 24/7/365.

At the Temple of Apollo in the ancient Greek town of Delphi, three maxims were carved at the entrance. One of them was, "Know thyself." It is widely regarded as the most important of the three maxims. It urges individuals to engage in introspection and self-reflection in order to gain a deeper understanding of their True Self.

To start this Discipline, you must let your freak flag fly, which means you are fully, unapologetically you in every situation.

When we are fully ourselves, we may appear quirky to others. The fact is that the world wants to judge us, and that dims our light. The sooner you shed your layers and decide to be yourself 100% of the time, the sooner you'll have more energy and shine bright. Because you won't have to fake it anymore. Being something you *are not* consumes a lot of energy.

As Marianne Williamson said in her famous quote, "It is our light, not our darkness, that most frightens us."

Knowing thyself is the gateway to fully being your True Self all the time. You will fully express yourself, acknowledging your weaknesses and capitalizing on your strengths.

For example, embracing the fact that I was an introvert was incredibly freeing. I have never liked small talk and social gatherings, and I always thought there was something wrong with me. When I acknowledged that I was just being the introvert I am, that acceptance was liberating.

The more you know yourself and live that way, the better you will function. You'll stop feeling apologetic for being who you are. You won't waste energy trying to be someone the world wants you to be.

Have you ever felt you are one person at work, one person at home, one person with your friends, and so on? You're trying to be all things to all people. The textbook example of this happened when my wife threw me a surprise thirtieth-birthday party. When I saw a hundred people yell, "Surprise!" I was first excited, then struck by a sinking feeling of "Holy cow! Who am I going to be today?"

That's because I could see six different factions of my life in one room. There were my employees and business partners. My family—mom, dad, brothers, and cousins. My wife's family.

My high school friends, entrepreneur friends, and friends from the neighborhood.

I realized I was a different person with each of these six groups of people. I was a chameleon! With my employees I was "boss Gino." With my high school friends I was "crazy Gino." With my new friends I was "less-crazy Gino." And so on.

It was a wake-up call, and from that day on I was "authentic Gino."

Imagine how much energy I was expending being who I thought I had to be with each individual group. Since that discovery I began shedding layers, as described in part I. And in the last few years since chopping away massive chunks of marble, I feel even more authentic and free.

Now I am simply myself with everyone. I am hardworking, hard-playing, funny, passionate, intense, loving, obsessive, introverted, gritty me. I've come to the realization that I'm just a big, sensitive, cushy love ball, and always was, under the tough-guy layers of armor my ego created at age fifteen. And just being a cushy love ball makes me feel so much lighter.

So who are you?

Consider this visualization. Close your eyes. Imagine that you are attending an industry conference. You are finished dressing in your hotel room and about to make your way to the preconference cocktail party. Check in with your body. What feelings and sensations come up for you?

Check in with your mind. What thoughts and emotions arise?

Now, imagine you are standing at the doorway to the cocktail party. You stop and survey a room of people standing at high-top tables engaged in conversation. You notice that you do not recognize anyone. Again, check in with your body. What feelings and sensations come up for you? Check in with your mind. What thoughts and emotions arise?

Now, imagine you have made your way into the room and walked up to a group of people you have never met before. You introduce yourself and start to engage in conversation. One more time, check in with your body. What feelings and sensations come up for you? Check in with your mind. What thoughts and emotions arise? Are you your True Self? Or are you a chameleon?

To build on this exercise, imagine a similar scenario, but this time you are making your way into a room of family or friends who love you unconditionally. Imagine you are standing at the doorway and surveying the roomful of people. Check in with your body. What feelings and sensations come up for you? Check in with your mind. What thoughts and emotions arise?

Now, imagine entering the room and walking up to a group of your family and friends. Check in with your body. What feelings and sensations come up for you? Check in with your mind. What thoughts and emotions arise? Are you your True Self?

Were you the same person, your True Self, in both scenarios? Were you a chameleon? Were you someone in between?

As the saying goes, "Hell on earth would be meeting the person you could have been."

The process of knowing thyself so you can fully be your True Self is that of understanding your skills and abilities, and realizing your strengths and weaknesses, along with shedding all layers to present the real you. The following are some of the many ways to do so.

You can use profiling tools like DiSC, Myers-Briggs, Culture Index, Kolbe A™ Index, or Enneagram to understand your skills, abilities, strengths, and weaknesses. I've taken at least ten different ones, and they've all had an impact on my clarity.

We typically do not recommend one profiling tool over another, but one of Rob's favorites is the Enneagram. It provides a whole-life view into yourself. Thousands of years old, its roots can be traced back to philosophical and spiritual traditions. While not scientific, it can be quite insightful. The foundation of the Enneagram is nine personality types we all have within us. You will learn which one is your dominant type, and that will provide you insight into the motivations that fuel your behavior.

Rob has seen people brought to tears as they unpack the generations of Enneagram types in their family that led them to why they are a certain way. It has a therapeutic aspect, as the tears give way to acceptance of their True Self.

Another way to know yourself better is to get therapy. It is aimed at relieving emotional distress and mental health problems. I've never met anyone who didn't need a little bit of guidance, just as Rob and I did. It is a great way to shed layers.

Randy McDougal, a successful entrepreneur, shares his experience: "For me, therapy has given me the freedom to be vulnerable and curious about life and relational difficulties. It has made me comfortable being me, instead of feeling like I have to prove to those around me that I'm 'okay.'

"Through therapy, I've learned to separate my value as a person from what I do or do not do. I learned how in early life I developed 'compensations' to help me get through challenges. While most of my compensations are socially acceptable (working hard, keeping busy, making money), they are distractions, and they can undermine me and those closest to me."

Randy also offers this advice: "Many people try one therapist and then give up. All therapists are not the same, and we each need to find the one who fits us and where we are in life right now."

There are many different types of therapy; here are five examples:

1. Cognitive-behavioral therapy: A form of talk therapy to help you manage your problems by changing how you think and behave.

2. Dialectical behavior therapy: A structured program of psychotherapy with a strong educational component designed to provide skills for managing intense emotions and negotiating social relationships.*

3. Humanistic therapy: This form of talk therapy assesses a person's individual nature, focusing on the whole person, their positive characteristics, and their potential for growth.†

---

* From *Psychology Today*, www.psychologytoday.com/us/therapy-types /dialectical-behavior-therapy.

† From *Psychology Today*, www.psychologytoday.com/us/therapy-types /humanistic-therapy.

4. Mindfulness-based therapy: A modified form of cognitive therapy incorporating mindfulness practices such as present-moment awareness, meditation, and breathing exercises.*

5. Psychedelic-assisted therapy: This type incorporates psychedelics to help facilitate deep personal insight and healing.

An additional way to know thyself better is to get honest feedback from the people in your life. We urge every client to ask those around them what they see as their strengths and weaknesses, and to ask what they do well and where they could improve.

When our clients do the "strengths and weaknesses" exercise, they often focus on their respondents' weakness feedback. Possibly like you, they are learners and passionate about improving themselves. But we encourage you to place greater energy on the strengths feedback. Your strengths are what make you unique and are how you will make an impact. Your weaknesses are simply things to be aware of—what are *not* your superpowers—and what you should avoid doing where possible.

Your strengths may include being a bit of a mad scientist who is brilliant at solving problems. Or you might ask the perfect question at the perfect time. Or you intuitively recognize a great opportunity that will take your business to a new level. These attributes are your superpowers. They are what make you special.

---

* From Castle Craig, www.castlecraig.co.uk/admissions/frequently-asked-questions/what-happens-in-residential-rehab/.

We also urge our clients to create a "Who Am I Statement." You write a short statement that describes you as a person, providing a picture of who you are, what is important to you, and what you stand for. It can be one sentence or a paragraph. To get your mind going, you can start by writing a list of your traits. Examples of traits include accepting, argumentative, athletic, brave, caring, cheerful, complex, daring, disagreeable, efficient, faithful, generous, hardworking, humble, independent, logical, mature, patriotic, realistic, strong, thoughtful, understanding, wild . . . and the list can go on and on.

A note of caution: your first swipe at this statement may not be accurate. A client of ours wrote the sentence, "I am a chameleon." She proudly shared that she had learned to change to meet the circumstances of any situation she found herself in. While this may seem like a good trait to some, I felt sad for her because, as I described earlier, that's what I had been. Imagine having to fit yourself into every situation by becoming someone who you are not. Again, this is why "knowing yourself" is the starting point of this Discipline. We are going to help you get to the real you.

For this exercise, begin thinking about what "I" means to you. This is a way to make this exercise more meaningful. Here are some examples of Who Am I Statements:

"I am ever wondering. I am open to the idea that I will never truly know who I am, and that's okay. I am here to learn. Every day is an opportunity, a small step forward, to learn more about who this body of constantly changing cells is. I am nothing, I am everything." —Rob Dube

"I am a being who observes thoughts, emotions, and experiences unfolding around me. I am interconnected, I am
love." —Michael McKinney

"I am a strong, beautiful soul in a human named Ginny
Wood. As such, I live in gratitude for simply being."
—Ginny Wood

As I mentioned, I am a cushy love ball who is hardworking, hard-playing, funny, passionate, intense, loving, obsessive,
introverted, and gritty.

Now, let's pull this entire chapter together and tie it to the
first half of this book, "The 3 Discoveries to Free Your True Self."

This chapter is about knowing thyself. If you *really* know
yourself, you can then be your True Self by chiseling away all
the unnecessary marble, and exposing the work of art that is you
to the world.

Once you realize that your True Self is in there, trapped
under that structure, this is your opportunity to remove it and
free your True Self.

We urge you to be patient but also urge you to start now.
This is what we were preparing you for in the first half of this
book. It is time for you to be free.

As promised, we have offered many ways to understand
your skills, abilities, strengths, weaknesses, and how to start to
shed layers in this chapter, but there are many more listed in
the "Resources for Shedding Layers" section in the back of this
book. Please review the list and see if any appeal to you.

I think I am up to more than thirty experiences I have benefited from over the previous twenty-five years, all of which are on the list, whether it was a book, therapist, event, facilitator, plant medicine, meditation, journaling, telling my inner story, or just processing on my own. They have all helped in some way. Remember, it's an unfolding journey.

Knowing thyself is always a work in progress. I don't know where I am toward fully becoming my True Self, but it just keeps getting better and better. We hope you'll join us on this journey.

Please commit to one step you will take in the next week to move closer to knowing thyself. Take one of the profiling tools. Or, schedule a session with a therapist. Send an email to the five people you are closest to and ask, "What are my three greatest strengths and my three greatest weaknesses?" You can also pick something from the "Resources for Shedding Layers."

CHAPTER SUMMARY

The Point

Be your True Self 100% of the time, 24/7/365.

Three Thought Prompts

1. What is one of your qualities that you have embraced over the years?
2. What is one of your qualities you have yet to embrace?
3. What is your Who Am I Statement?

_____

_____

_____

_____

_____

_____

_____

_____

_____

_____

_____

_____

_____

BE STILL

The main point of this Discipline is:

Sit in silence for thirty minutes every day.

As an entrepreneur, you go hard all day, every day. But at certain times you must stop. Literally put on the brakes and just breathe.

I have been amazed at how closing my eyes and breathing deeply shift me out of my head and into my body. It centers me. It helps create clarity on the project I'm working on, or the problem I'm trying to solve. For instance, as I was writing this book, my best ideas came when I was still every morning for thirty minutes.

Someone taught me a metaphor to illustrate the power of stillness. Imagine a glass jar full of water and a little bit of sand. Imagine shaking that jar. The water will be cloudy, murky, and unclear—like most of us when we go, go, go all day, every day. But if you let the glass jar sit for a few minutes, the sand settles, and the water becomes clear and calm. Just like what will happen with your mind and body if you are still for a few minutes.

Again, this is another opportunity to stop and let everything in your life catch up and sink in.

This Discipline will greatly increase your energy. You will feel like you just drank a cup of coffee, but without the jitters or the caffeine crash sixty minutes later.

Again, the energy we're referring to is not the usual type. It doesn't involve your stamina to do things, although that will increase. We are referring to the ball of energy that is you shining brighter and vibrating higher. Being still will also increase your inner peace while creating the space and time you need to shed layers and sculpt yourself.

You can use your time in stillness in several ways. The four forms of stillness we suggest are meditation, prayer, journaling, and contemplation. You can choose one or more as part of your routine. (These are not the only ways, so please find what works best for you.)

For most driven people, taking time to be still is very difficult and scary. This is simply fear and, as we've shared, you can go to the root of that fear and remove it, just by sitting with it.

The Four Forms of Stillness

Meditation

Many people choose this form of stillness. I spend thirty to sixty minutes most mornings meditating. Rob's routine is forty-five minutes in the morning when he wakes and twenty minutes in the evening prior to bed.

Meditation is a simple practice, yet it can seem daunting to many. The main point to understand about meditation is that you are not trying to free yourself from your thoughts. In fact, you'll be thinking most of the time. When you notice your thoughts, you simply let them go and return to focusing on your breath or a mantra. This will restore your awareness of the present moment.

Rob teaches the following steps for mindfulness meditation:

1. Find a comfortable seat on a chair or meditation cushion.
2. Sit upright, comfortably.
3. Place your hands gently on your legs.
4. If you are seated on a chair, and this is comfortable, move your back off the back of the chair so you are seated in a self-supported position, and bring your attention to the sensation of your feet firmly planted on the ground.
5. If you are on a meditation cushion, bring your attention to your bottom, firmly planted on the cushion.
6. Bring your attention to your hands, noticing the sensation of your hands resting gently on your legs.

7. Bring your attention to your posture: sitting upright, not too rigid, not too soft. Somewhere in the middle that is comfortable.

8. Tilt your chin down slightly.

9. Close your eyes or keep your eyes open with a soft gaze four to six feet in front of you.

10. Bring your attention to your breath, breathing in and out naturally. Nothing special.

11. Notice the sensation of the air as it enters your nostrils.

12. Continue to breathe in and out naturally, following the path of your breath.

13. After a few minutes, you may notice you've been carried away in a train of thought. That is normal. Once you notice it, simply bring your attention back to your breath, breathing in and out naturally, following the path of your breath.

14. After a few more minutes, you may notice you are, again, lost in thought. When you notice you are thinking, allow the thoughts to go by, like clouds in the sky or waves in the ocean. You can say "thinking" and bring your attention back to your breath. The present moment. Right here, right now.

15. At the end of your meditation, sit quietly for a moment. Bring your attention back to the sensation of your feet on the ground or your bottom on the cushion and your hands on your legs. Open your eyes and reorient yourself to your surroundings. Take a deep breath and bring this feeling with you throughout your day.

This is just one of many ways to meditate. There are countless books and online videos on various other methods. You have to discover your own best way.

You can also use one of the many meditation apps that will guide you through meditation, including the following six:

- Insight Timer
- Meditation Studio App
- Waking Up
- 10% Happier
- Headspace
- Calm

Meditation has been very profound for me. I believe it has provided the greatest benefit in terms of becoming my True Self, shedding layers, and finding inner peace. I have shed many layers during my meditation. I also believe it has greatly helped my ability to stay calm in the "real world" and has given me great clarity. A friend of mine who meditates regularly shared a funny story with me. When he drives his kids to school, he occasionally gets frustrated in traffic. When he vocalizes it, his kids ask, "Dad, did you miss your meditation practice today?"

Prayer

For many, prayer connects them to a higher power. It is a reminder to let go and experience a deeper sense of connection. It also may be a time to make requests, such as for the strength to make it through a challenging situation or guidance on a decision one is contemplating.

Leaders of all religions emphasize the importance of making prayer a regular part of a person's life. A common theme among them is that it can be transformative to connect with a higher power and deepen one's relationship with it, leading to greater compassion, self-awareness, and peace.

Mahatma Gandhi said, "Prayer is not asking. It's a longing of the soul. It is daily admission of one's weaknesses. It is better in prayer to have a heart without words than words without a heart."

Journaling

Journaling is another form of being still. Many find it therapeutic to get their deep thoughts onto a piece of paper. Maya Angelou famously said, "There is no greater agony than bearing an untold story inside you."

Find a quiet place with no distractions (music, television, phone, etc.) and start letting your hand move. Do not overthink or stop. Some call it "hot penning." It allows your conscious mind to let go and your subconscious to take over. Reading what you wrote in your journal can help create clarity, identify patterns and themes in your life, provide perspective, and bring greater self-awareness. On the other hand, Rob journals every day and intentionally does not go back to read his entries. Ultimately, it is up to you to determine what works best.

Patricia Karpas, cofounder of the Meditation Studio App and the podcast *Untangle*, along with her business partner

Cyd Crouse, shares that journaling has been an important daily practice for her for more than forty years. Each morning at six o'clock, she spends fifteen minutes journaling about thoughts, feelings, and experiences of the previous day, the miscellaneous ideas swirling around in her head, and anything top of mind. At the end, she takes a minute to practice gratitude, listing all the gifts of the day and in her life, big and small. Patricia's daily journaling is accompanied by her meditation practice. She treasures this time as a way to cultivate self-awareness and compassion, as well as to reflect and contemplate. She likes to take time to focus on what matters most, versus any daily annoyances that might be tugging at her.

Journaling was part of what motivated Patricia to leave a frenetic media career and become a social entrepreneur. Her goal was to have a greater impact on the world by making meditation more accessible to all. She doesn't like to reread her journals, "perhaps because they're so much a reflection of the 'moments' that are in the past. Why go back?"

Journaling prompts are a way to jump-start your mind. Below are four you may find useful to get your journaling practice going:

- Challenges: Looking at yourself from the outside, as if you were another person, what are the three or four most important challenges in your life currently?
- Self: Write down three or four important facts about yourself. What accomplishments have you achieved? What skills or good qualities do you have?

- Intention: Reflect on your 10-Year Thinking Vision. Now think about what you want to leave behind when you are no longer on this earth. Bring clarity to what you want to create. What do you want to do to achieve that? Does your 10-Year Thinking Vision incorporate it?
- Letting go: What would you have to let go of (behaviors, thought processes, blocks) in order to bring your 10-Year Thinking Vision into reality? What layers do you need to shed?

Contemplation

When you contemplate, you find stillness and reflect on your understanding of yourself and the world around you. Meister Eckhart, the German theologian, philosopher, and mystic, emphasized the divine "spark" in each person. He said, "What we plant in the soil of contemplation, we shall reap in the harvest of action." He taught that an individual, through contemplation and meditation, is able to transcend their ego and become united with the divine, which leads to a deeper understanding of one's true nature.

To contemplate, find a quiet, comfortable spot. A friend of Rob's has a comfortable chair that faces a huge willow tree in his backyard. Each morning, for twenty minutes, he watches the willow tree swaying in the wind. Just watching the movements provides him with peace. He found it especially useful while he was dealing with a challenging health issue. As you sit, you can reflect on your thoughts and emotions and observe them without judgment. This is not a time to solve problems, as that will come later.

Let Stuff Come Up

In addition to the many benefits of stillness, like reduced stress, better focus, increased awareness, improved health, and more energy and creativity, you also create space for doing inner world work. In that stillness you will have a level of clarity you have never experienced before. This clarity may shock you. You may begin to realize you're in the wrong business. You may realize you need to fire a client or make a change to your leadership team. Maybe you will be inspired to change the purpose of your business altogether to one that will inspire your team, your customers, and the world.

In your personal life, you may begin to realize that you have been living too much on the adrenaline from your business. You may decide to sell your business so you can spend more time on a greater cause, or with the people who mean the most to you and maybe repair relationships that have suffered due to your driven nature. Imagine you start to see the world through a new lens and begin to find joy in areas of your life that you didn't know was possible. This joy may arise from activities like taking walks in nature or joining friends in a pickleball league.

Taking time every day to be still creates space in your mind to keep doing the inside work. This is what we were preparing you for in the first half of this book. In stillness, things will come up that have been blocked. This can be difficult and painful for some. If it's too much, I recommend that you seek professional help. If you are able to allow these things to come up, let them arise without judgment or trying to solve anything. If you notice you are judging or solving, come back to the present moment with the knowledge that you are okay and don't have to do anything right now. Treat yourself with warmth, care, and humor, and allow any feelings to exit. Remember the "Process One" exercise we taught you in Discovery #2, where you identify the emotions, location, shape, and color of past traumas? Apply that here when necessary. It should be quite helpful.

Over time, as you make your way through your day, you will begin to notice, as a result of your stillness practice, the effects of your life experiences, pain, or trauma that have shaped some of your unhealthy thinking and actions. As a result, your awareness will soar.

Remember, decisions are made out of love or fear. These include emotions, thoughts, and reactions. You will notice all the "stuff" that comes up, and you can unblock it and let it go.

You also will become more mindful in your day-to-day interactions with people. For instance, when a family member or coworker makes a remark that triggers you, you will recognize the emotion welling up inside of you as based in fear. This is your awareness at work. In the past, you might have reacted with a negative outburst. Now, however, you can pause, breathe, and respond, having seen exactly what triggered you after something hit your "stuff." You can then go to the block and process it. Being triggered always comes from an upset place inside you. People's words should never affect us. As Viktor Frankl famously said, "Between stimulus and response, there is a space. In that space is our power to choose our response. In our response lies our growth and our freedom." This is the freedom for you to be your True Self.

Spending time in stillness gives you the opportunity to learn how to just be. Once you develop this ability, you can extend that into all aspects of your life. You can just be when you are at home, when you are with friends and family, when you are at work. And the more you just be, the more you will actually do. Now that's impact and peace.

Tomorrow morning, before you start your day, sit quietly in a chair. Be still. Pause and breathe. Take at least ten minutes for starters. See what happens. Do this for thirty days and see for yourself. Slowly move up to thirty minutes based on your comfort level. It will have an incredible impact on your energy, your mood, and your relationships.

CHAPTER SUMMARY

The Point

Sit in silence for thirty minutes every day.

Three Thought Prompts

1. Write down one to three reasons why it is hard for you to be still.

2. Set a timer and close your eyes for one minute. Imagine what it would be like to be still for thirty minutes. After the minute is up, write down what sensations you were feeling in your body. Write down what emotions came up for you.

3. Look at your calendar and schedule the best time to be still daily.

_____

_____

_____

_____

_____

_____

_____

_____

_____

KNOW YOUR 100%

The main point of this Discipline is:

*Decide on and commit to the perfect number
of hours per week and weeks per year that you
will deliver your impact to the world.*

Think of your 100% as your "work container." To maximize your impact, you must decide your perfect number of working hours that will produce your peak energy. Pinpoint the amount of time at which literally one more hour of work would be less fun or start burning you out, and one fewer hour would start to bore you or make you feel like you weren't doing enough.

This is the inverse of Discipline #2: Take Time Off. They are two sides of the same coin but very different from each other.

One is about fully recharging your batteries, and the other is about determining your maximum output and impact.

Think about your ideal time to start work and what time you prefer to stop working, along with how many days a week you want to work and how many weeks per year. This Discipline, when followed religiously, maximizes your energy.

As a driven entrepreneur, you are capable of making an incredible impact in this world. Aristotle said it perfectly: "Where your talents and the needs of the world cross lies your calling."

You have learned that the better you understand who you are, the more you will be yourself and make the most impact. With each Discipline, you are creating more and more clarity. You are opening up greater space in your life, which provides you the creativity needed to understand, intuitively, the best way for you to uniquely make that impact.

To illustrate, Meg Mayhugh runs her own consulting firm, and she has been on the leadership team of several other companies as the head of HR or of growth. She lives by this Discipline. She has an extraordinary gift for helping people understand how to leverage their time, both through her coaching and by her example. She is a single parent of three kids and works hard to protect her 100%. She is not afraid to ask for assistance. She delegates tasks unapologetically so that she can be a hockey coach, volunteer board member at a local nonprofit, and lifeguard. Juggling her tasks is not always easy, but she makes it look that way.

I work forty weeks per year and fifty hours per week. My work day typically starts at eight o'clock and ends at six o'clock. In between, I go very hard and love it.

Rob's 100% is forty-three weeks per year and forty-five hours per week. This enables him to follow a daily routine of waking at 5 AM for forty-five minutes of meditation, ten minutes of journaling, and twenty minutes of contemplative reading, followed by yoga/stretching and a run. He's ready and in his home office by eight-thirty. On most days, between 12:30 PM and 1:30 PM, he has lunch with his wife, followed by a walk, and is back at it no later than two. His day ends by 6:30 PM after twenty minutes of preparing for tomorrow.

Those are the perfect 100%s for us. What is your perfect 100%?

At times, you will not be able to work within your perfect number. You may be working on a large project or starting a new company, or maybe you got hit with a major issue or anything else that may require you to exceed your set boundaries. While understandable, this should only be a rare exception. There is a saying: "You can live out of balance as long as you know for how long and why." Keep this in mind and stay focused on getting back to your ideal work capacity as soon as possible before you burn out.

Maximum Output

When I was teaching the concept of knowing your 100%, one gentleman compared it to the gauge in a car that shows the maximum fuel efficiency based on how hard you press the accelerator. It's the same principle. It's your maximum energy efficiency: how you get the most personal miles per gallon from your internal fuel.

Here's an example of how to get the most impact out of your 100%. If you are most energized by selling and working with customers, imagine spending 100% of your working time focused on doing that. What would that do to your energy?

Now, imagine if only 10% of your working time was selling and working with customers and the other 90% was administrative work. What would that do to your energy? Please stop and ponder those two scenarios for a minute. The idea is to shift to spending most of your work container on the work that energizes you the most.

If you don't protect the amount of time you want to work and what goes on inside of your work container, where does work end? If work hours and activities are negotiable, then you'll always operate above your 100% and have less energy, and you'll get burned out. You won't be the best version of yourself.

Entrepreneur Jim Rohn said, "Time is our most valuable asset, yet we tend to waste it, kill it, and spend it rather than invest it."

Once you are clear about your work container, you will begin the process of doing only the things you love to do and delegating everything else. Then you will only be doing the things that give you energy. Let's call these True Self Activities. You'll begin to experience a freedom you lacked before. This freedom creates energy, sparks your creativity, puts you in a flow state, and naturally leads you to focus on only doing things that make a greater impact. Remember the concept of no time we mentioned under the 10-Year Thinking Discipline? When you concentrate solely on your True Self Activities, it's as if time is standing still. You are Flowting!

Being more impactful requires doing less. In a *Wall Street Journal* piece by Rachel Feintzeig, she shares the story of Bevin Mugford, who was working up to ninety hours per week helping to pivot her business. As sales increased, she felt an adrenaline rush, sharing that "you get addicted." Yet she began to find herself growing so exhausted that one day she could not get out of bed. Bevin was burned out. She had no choice but to build boundaries in her work life. She took time off to meditate, journal, and go to therapy. She stopped scheduling her regular 6 AM meetings, started taking a downtime break during the workday, and now ends her days at 4:55 PM to head to the gym without taking calls. "It was in the quiet," she says, "that I figured out how to reprioritize my time." You may have noticed that Bevin's story illustrates the power of bringing all of the Disciplines together. My hope is that you will incorporate this Discipline into your life so you do not have to experience the pain that she did.

Once you have determined your perfect number of hours per week and weeks per year, you may notice that you cannot fit everything into that time frame. We will explain more in the next two chapters about how to remove excess baggage and concentrate your attention on the most important activities that make the greatest impact.

As you decide on the size of your work container, please be patient. You will have to experiment to find your perfect number of hours and days. Keep this in mind if you find yourself becoming frustrated or overstimulated.

To determine your perfect number of hours per week and weeks per year, and what your True Self Activities are, complete this exercise:

- Look at the last two to three months of your calendar for reference and to spark your creativity. Notice the things you did that gave you energy (True Self Activities) and those that didn't.
- Draw three columns on a piece of paper titled "Gives energy," "Drains energy," and "Not sure." Write each of your work-related activities in the appropriate column.
- Write down the names of one to three people and/or one to three things that consistently intrude on your work–life boundaries. Include thoughts on how you can eliminate these.
- Write down your 100%, your perfect number of hours per week. If you are stuck, pick both a number that seems like too much and a number that seems like not enough. Then pick a number in the middle to get started.
- Write down the perfect number of weeks per year that you feel maximizes your energy. Use the days-off exercise in Discipline #2: Take Time Off as a way to back into this.

CHAPTER SUMMARY

The Point

Decide on and commit to the perfect number of hours per week and weeks per year that you will deliver your impact to the world.

Three Thought Prompts

1. Are your perfect number of hours per week and weeks per year aligned with your 10-Year Thinking?
2. Write down a time when you were overwhelmed in your work life. Notice the sensations in your body. Notice the emotions you feel. Write them down.
3. Write down a time you were in Flowt in your work life. Notice the sensations in your body. Notice the emotions you feel. Write them down.

_____

_____

_____

_____

_____

_____

_____

_____

_____

SAY NO ... OFTEN

The main point of this Discipline is:

*Say no to everything that doesn't fit
into the first five Disciplines.*

With the first five Disciplines in place, this one becomes easy. Your long-range vision is now clear, your time commitments are determined, you are taking time to be still every day, and you know who you are. With this clarity, your boundaries are illuminated and it's now obvious what you should not be doing.

In *Essentialism: The Disciplined Pursuit of Less*, a great book on the subject of simplifying your life, author Greg McKeown addresses the necessity of saying no. He states, "The very thought of saying no literally brings us physical discomfort. We feel guilty." He adds, "Either we can say no and regret it for a few minutes, or we can say yes and regret it for days, weeks, months, or even years."

McKeown also shares a great principle on how you should filter your decisions: "If it isn't a clear *yes*, then it's a clear *no*."

You will learn how to say no with good intentions and kindness, all while being helpful to the person asking. For example, Rob regularly reaches out to well-known people with a humble request for them to be a guest on his podcast, *Leading with Genuine Care*. The best-known people often respond with a thoughtful no, but even the turn-down brings a smile to Rob's face. One prospective guest, Adam Grant, a Wharton School professor and *New York Times* best-selling author whose TED talks have more than twenty-five million views, responded to Rob's request with the following message:

"Thanks, Rob—honored that my work resonated, and I appreciate the invite. Unfortunately, my plate is beyond full, but please let me know if I can recommend other guests for you."

Rob responded: "Many thanks for the response and consideration. Saying no is an important quality! I will take you up on your offer to recommend others. Feel free to email me, and I'll take it from here. If I can ever be useful to you, please let me know."

Within ninety minutes, Adam responded to Rob with a list of eight potential guests. He was intentional, kind, and useful. Saying yes to being a guest on the podcast would have cost him the time to prepare for the appearance, be interviewed (at least an hour), and return to his own work—about two hours, which he instead used for high-energy, high-impact priorities.

Another example is Dan Harris, the former ABC News anchor, another *New York Times* best-seller, and creator of the app 10% Happier. Rob first reached out to Dan years ago to request that he appear on *Leading with Genuine Care*.

Dan took two minutes to respond: "Hey Rob, Thanks for the kind words. Sadly, I am going to have to pass, as I am on a deadline for my next book and am turning down most invitations."

Rob followed up two years later, and Dan had this response: "Thanks so much, Rob! Really appreciate the resource and tips. Sadly, I am going to pass on the pod yet again, as I continue to jealously guard my time, given the onslaught. Continued good luck on your work."

A year later, Rob received this reply: "Hey, I really appreciate your persistence. Hate to keep letting you down, but I'm still very aggressively trying to keep my schedule clear for writing."

And, a year after that: "Rob, happy new year! And thanks as always for the gentle persistence. Sadly, not much has changed on my end in the intervening year. I'm still thigh deep in the writing process and working feverishly to protect my time. I'm doing very few outside interviews. I hope to have the book done in 12–18 months, then published around this time in two years. How about I make a promise to give you an interview when the book comes out?"

Over a period of four years, Dan took fewer than ten minutes to respond to Rob's emails kindly. He finally saw a benefit to potentially saying yes at some point when his book would be released. He later recommended an outstanding guest for Rob's podcast, which was beneficial to both Rob and to Dan's company, 10% Happier. A win-win, and it took Dan just three more minutes.

Remember when we discussed making your decisions out of love or fear? When you say yes to someone, are you doing it out of FOMO—fear of missing out—on the next potential big opportunity because you said no? Are you afraid you are going to disappoint someone because you said no? Are you afraid you would feel guilty if you said no? Do you say yes to have a minute of peace or relief? If you answered yes to any of those questions, you are making your decisions out of fear.

By becoming your True Self, you begin making decisions from the inside out versus the outside in. It will be abundantly clear with this approach when to say yes or no. This requires self-awareness. You can probably recall a time you made a commitment, but when you had to fulfill it, you found yourself annoyed, rushed, anxious, or out of alignment. If you are saying yes to things that prevent you from spending time on things that make an impact, you should not be doing them. If you are spending time on things that do not fulfill you, you should not be doing them. These choices harm our mental and physical well-being.

Sometimes we allow external forces to influence our decisions (outside in). Please do not let these overshadow your inner wisdom and values. When you are making decisions from the inside out, you are finding what it means to be balanced and aligned with your True Self. You are using your intuition.

Here's how this works in practice. Michael McKinney had been a longtime member of a leading trade association in his industry. The CEO of the association recognized him as a young leader and asked him to serve on the group's Education Committee. The time Michael would have to spend on this didn't fit well with his schedule or efforts to build his business, but he let ego and FOMO rule his decision.

Yet during the very first meeting, he regretted accepting the assignment. The meetings were done via conference calls, which was clunky and often led to time overruns. Even worse, the work was unfulfilling, as it focused on revenue generated for the association from education rather than the education itself. He stuck with it for the rest of the term but was glad when it ended. Michael eventually realized the power of saying no, and when asked to run for the board of directors of the same association, he kindly declined, explaining that his workload and family were filling his time.

Most driven people want to be liked, which is often why they say yes. For Nate Klemp of Mindful, the most powerful external factor can be distilled to a single word: "guilt." Because of guilt, he feels that he should say yes to a business trip, so he goes. Because of guilt, he feels that he should say yes to a family obligation, so he goes. Learning how to say no has been a matter of learning how to accept guilty feelings while standing firm.

You might feel the same guilt, pain, or discomfort inside when someone requests something of you. You think you are solving your pain by saying yes and feeling temporary peace, but in the end you end up feeling regret.

There are many teachings on the power of saying yes. Some say it helps you build your network and relationships. Others say that giving someone a yes means they will do something for you. Still others say that you "never know what might happen." All of these reasons are legitimate, but if you subscribe to this philosophy, make sure you pause, check in with yourself, and consider if the yes will bring you energy and allow you to make a greater impact in the world. If you'd otherwise be sitting around twiddling your thumbs, you probably should say yes. But the typical driven entrepreneur is usually not so idle.

At this point in your career, usually you will be fortunate enough to have many opportunities—often, more than you know what to do with. Warren Buffett said it well: "The difference between successful people and *really* successful people is that *really* successful people say no to almost everything."

Consider this scenario. A friend calls you to say she is involved with a well-respected nonprofit in your community. She is energized by their purpose and the work they are doing. They are adding board members and, because she has such respect for you, she asks if you might be interested. She goes on to share how you would be an asset to the board because of your unique skill set. Would it be okay for her to connect you with Bob, the nonprofit's executive director? You say yes. After all, you don't want to let your friend down, and you aren't committing to anything other than chatting with Bob.

Your friend connects the two of you. Bob emails that he would like to treat you at a favorite coffee shop of his. You originally thought this would be a phone call but decide that meeting for coffee might be nice, so you agree. The two of you exchange emails to find a date, and Bob shares the location, a thirty-five-minute drive downtown for you.

The day before the meeting, you see it on your calendar and have a minor regret as you are forgoing your morning workout to drive downtown (thirty-five minutes), need time to find parking (ten minutes), and like to be ten minutes early (total fifty-five minutes). You arrive at the coffee shop the next day early as planned. Unfortunately, Bob is running late and rushes in, frazzled and apologetic, ten minutes past your scheduled time. By the time he grabs his coffee and the two of you settle in, thirty minutes have already passed. Still, Bob is charismatic, and you are drawn into his message, so the meeting runs fifteen minutes late. At the end, Bob compliments you on all your successes and lets you know he would be honored if you joined their board. You pause and say yes.

As you rush back to your office, a thirty-five-minute drive, you realize you are late for a client visit and call in to let the team know. Unfortunately, this series of events, from your friend contacting you through your meeting with Bob, is just the beginning of the consequences of your yes.

You join the board and quickly learn that it entails a three-year commitment, involving a great deal of preparation, time in meetings and on committees, fundraising pressure, and event planning and participation. Now, if you love the nonprofit, it gives you energy, and it supports the type of impact you want to make in the world, then yes is the right answer. Otherwise, it's a no.

Sadly, too many people have fallen into this pattern. Their yes was well intentioned, but they didn't think the consequences through. If they had said no, it would have saved hours of time—time they could have used to make a bigger impact.

Saying yes from love means you are clear about how much time you have and what gives you energy, which enables you to make the greatest impact. So check in with yourself before saying yes. Remember Daniel White, who does energy clearing? He advises, "You will feel a knowing when the yes is right, and a sensation when it should be a no." This is your intuition being fully online. This is you being aware. This is you making fewer fear-based decisions and more love-based decisions.

All of the Disciplines are interconnected and assist you in setting boundaries. When they are working together, the boundaries become very clear. Examples of Say No Often boundaries are:

- no meetings before 8:30 AM or after 5 PM
- no email on Saturdays or Sundays
- no lending money to friends
- no doing housework (hire someone)
- no running meetings
- no taking a meeting with someone I haven't been introduced to by someone I trust
- no more than four hours of meetings per day
- no back-to-back meetings
- no saying yes to things out of guilt

Make a list of your own Say No Often boundaries by listing five requests that do not work for you. Then start walking away from all the things that don't fit. The decision becomes as clear as someone asking you to eat a worm. You'd say no without hesitation. Every decision can be that easy. This applies to both your professional and your personal lives.

Dr. Jim Lewerenz, CEO of the Longevity Health Institute and a client, shared an impactful story of his father, a well-respected and beloved doctor in southeast Michigan. He touched thousands of lives in his thirty-year medical career. He was the physician for multiple Rock & Roll Hall of Famers as well as seven world boxing champions as the team physician for the world-famous Kronk Boxing Team. Jim's father said yes to many requests and, as a result, was involved with many patients. He was not good at saying no. While it didn't cause him anxiety, it did leave him without peace, joy, and happiness in his later years. He encouraged Jim not to let that happen to him as well.

By setting Say No Often boundaries, you will reduce the guilt you feel by saying no, because they make your reason for saying no obvious. You will stop doing things outside your True Self Activities. You'll no longer get sucked into doing activities that drain your energy.

Now, let's do a checkup. When you say no, how comfortable are you? Answer the following questions with a yes or no to gauge your "say no" comfort.

- Does saying no bring you physical discomfort? Y/N
- Do you regularly say yes to things that aren't a clear yes and regret it? Y/N
- Do you need to set criteria to help you decide when to say no? Y/N

- Do you experience FOMO (fear of missing out)? Y/N
- Do you feel guilty when you say no? Y/N
- Do you say yes to things that drain your energy? Y/N
- When you say yes, are you underestimating the value of your time? Y/N
- Does saying yes prevent you from focusing on something that's more important? Y/N
- Do you say yes to requests that don't align with your values, beliefs, and goals? Y/N
- Do you say yes to be liked? Y/N

The goal of these questions is to make you aware of your decision-making state: love based or fear based. For those questions to which you answered yes, take steps to become more comfortable answering no to them. To start, as you make your way through this coming week, consider committing to saying no to at least one person's request.

CHAPTER SUMMARY

The Point

Say no to everything that doesn't fit into the first five Disciplines.

Three Thought Prompts

1. For two minutes, picture your life where you say *yes* to most things. Write down two or three sensations you had in your body and two or three emotions that came up for you.

2. For two minutes, picture your life where you say *no* to most things. Write down two or three sensations you had in your body and two or three emotions that came up for you.

3. Write down three things in the last ninety days you agreed to do when you should have said no. Did you make the decision out of fear? Did it align with everything you learned in the first five Disciplines? Did you make your decision from the inside out or the outside in?

_____

_____

_____

_____

_____

_____

DON'T DO $25-AN-HOUR WORK

The main point of this Discipline is:

Never do anything you could pay someone $25 an hour to do.

We're not knocking this type of work, and we're not knocking people who do that work. We all need people making $25 an hour, because that makes the economy run. If you are happy making $25 an hour, that's wonderful. But we're assuming the reader of this book is either making or wants to make six figures or more, as most driven entrepreneurs do. If so, then you shouldn't be doing $25-an-hour work.

To start, you must eliminate all administrative tasks from your life. You shouldn't be checking emails, opening mail, managing your calendar, scheduling appointments, booking travel, or doing follow-up and follow-through work. Those tasks drain your energy. You must delegate them all.

This type of work holds you back from gaining the freedom in your life that will spark your creativity and lead to you making a satisfying impact in this world. Your focus should be on high-energy, high-impact work.

Take checking your own email, for example. I dread responding to email. It distracts me and saps my energy. As a result, I have not managed my daily email in more than fifteen years. My solution was simple: my assistant does it. You can do the same. Get an assistant to do your administrative tasks so you can spend all of your time in your personal sweet spot, doing the things you determined were your True Self, high-impact, most valuable, high-energy activities.

Many driven Visionaries have a difficult time letting go of email. That condemns them to hundreds of emails per day, among which those needing a response are overwhelmed by a combination of junk and informational notes. Email is out of control. Most people need two to four hours per day to keep up, and many end up clearing out their emails from their phone while in bed at night. It's stressful knowing an avalanche of requests, questions, information, and the like is waiting for your attention.

Many of our clients share that, prior to learning how to effectively delegate this task, they believed only they could manage their emails. They couldn't wrap their minds around how someone else could respond in the unique way that they felt only they could. How, they wondered, could an assistant determine which email is and isn't important? We promise our clients that the right assistant can.

Here is my email system. Once you have an assistant in place, share it with them. There are three types of email: junk email, informational email, and response email.

- Junk email: This one is easy; your assistant clears all of it so you never have to see it.
- Informational email: Teach your assistant which informational email you want to see and how you want to see it. Rob has his assistant move them into a subfolder called "informational email," where he reviews them every three to four weeks when he has time.
- Response email: This one scares people the most. For this category, your assistant should be able to respond to a minimum of 50 percent of these emails after thirty days of training. The other 50 percent or so you will handle.

Using this system, you will greatly reduce your time spent on email and will have a clearer mind. I believe it saves me fifteen hours per week.

What other types of tasks can you delegate? One driven Visionary entrepreneur of a fast-growing international shipping company was still reviewing and approving every invoice before it went out. His executive assistant walked into the Visionary's office late one night as he was poring over the invoices and asked, "Why are you doing that?"

"Because I'm the owner."

She replied, "It takes you two hours a day, it makes you upset, and honestly, you are not very good at it. Let me do it."

They put a process in place where she would approve anything under $50,000, and he would approve anything above. This freed up almost ten hours a week for the Visionary to focus on growing the company. What could you do with ten extra hours?

Other examples of $25-an-hour tasks related to work are:

- calendar management
- booking business travel
- meeting notes
- bookkeeping
- managing social media
- paperwork
- reporting
- ordering gifts
- vendor research

Don't feel guilty delegating these tasks. Many people want to do this work for you, and they enjoy doing it. It's their True Self activity. It gives them energy, and that is how they make an impact. Think of it this way: hiring someone to do these tasks helps the economy. In 2020, the Small Business Administration estimated that entrepreneurs employ 50 percent of the workforce in the United States.

Josh Kaufman, author of *The First 20 Hours: How to Learn Anything . . . Fast* and other best-sellers, says, "For everything we don't like to do, there is someone out there who is really good, wants to do it, and will enjoy it."

You also reap a direct financial benefit by avoiding $25-an-hour work, as exemplified in this quote from best-selling author, coach, and speaker John Maxwell: "If you want to do a few small things right, do them yourself. If you want to do great things and make a big impact, learn to delegate." In my thirty years of delegating this work, I have calculated a 5-to-1 return, usually within a year. By delegating the $25-an-hour work, I make $125 an hour. By delegating $100-an-hour work, I make $500 an hour. To me, that's a no-brainer!

How did I come up with those figures? Let's say you make $500,000 per year. Your hourly rate is approximately $250 per hour (based on a forty-hour workweek). If you are spending fifteen of your forty hours per week doing $25-an-hour work, you could be making approximately $200,000 more per year, assuming you replace that time with high-impact, high-return activities.

Besides the financial benefit of delegating these tasks, you gain the great benefit of enhanced freedom, creativity, energy, and peace. You now have more time in your life—say, ten more hours to sell, build an amazing team, talk to clients, do research and development, or work on yourself. At the very top of the scale, it can also lead to a game-changing idea for your business.

The same applies in your home life. Many years ago, when Rob purchased his first house, he would mow the lawn every weekend. He thought that was what a homeowner was supposed to do, even though he hated every moment of it. Then he learned he could pay a lawn service to do the work. Although he wasn't making much money at the time, he intuitively knew that spending quality time, fully present with his family, was worth every dollar he was spending. That's a basic example. If you love mowing your lawn and doing yard work, if it brings you peace and energy, keep doing it! But keep in mind that many of our non-work life tasks are energy draining. Things like:

- mowing the lawn
- shoveling snow
- handiwork around the house
- paying bills
- scheduling doctor appointments and managing medical details
- booking personal travel
- grocery shopping
- cleaning

Rob's administrative assistant created a system to have all the annual home "checkup" items for his house completed so he does not have to think about it. His assistant sets it all up. No more beeping smoke alarms at 3 AM! Instead, his assistant hires a handyman to regularly change the batteries. She also schedules his annual physical as well as any pre- or post-medical appointments.

Booking travel is a subject we like to have fun with when we teach this Discipline. Do you book your own travel? If you are like most people, you start by thinking it's not that difficult or time consuming. You just hop on the internet or the airline app and quickly purchase the ticket. The same with the hotel. And the rental car. Oh, and you want to use points, so you find yourself calculating and transferring points. The next thing you know, you've spent ninety minutes booking everything.

At first, some of our clients don't believe someone could understand all of their unique travel needs. Plus, they often felt guilty delegating non-work travel, especially when it involved other family members. But once they see the power of delegation, they feel free. An administrative assistant can quickly learn your unique travel requirements, such as only liking morning flights, preferring aisle seats, and needing a hotel in a quiet area. They also learn when to use points or pay in dollars. Once they start delegating travel planning, our clients share that the assistant does a *better* job than they do.

The workforce of today is flexible. It is easier than ever to find an assistant, no matter how many hours you need. Plenty of talented people work from home, and they would be happy to work as little as ten hours a week for you. If you need help finding and managing the hire, there are virtual assistant companies that will set you up.

Our core message in this Discipline: don't do low-energy, low-impact work. This book is all about freeing you and maximizing your impact and peace.

Here's how to get started:

- Write a list of all of the work-life administrative (low-energy, low-impact) tasks you are doing and how many hours it takes to get each done per week. Total the hours it takes to complete all of the tasks.

- Write a list of all of the non-work-life administrative (low-energy, low-impact) tasks you are doing and how many hours it takes to get each done per week. Total the hours it takes to complete all of the tasks.

- Using both lists, circle those tasks that drain your energy or don't make an impact.
- Write down your annual compensation. Using your perfect number of hours per week and weeks per year from Discipline #5: Know Your 100%, calculate your hourly rate. For example, let's say your annual compensation is $300,000. Your 100% is 45 weeks × 50 hours per week = 2,250 hours per year. $300,000 divided by 2,250 hours per year = $133.33 per hour.
- Now, add up the hours the tasks from your work life and non-work life take you to complete (e.g., 15 hours). Multiply the number of hours by your hourly rate ($133.33). The annual cost of your time doing that work is nearly $90,000 (15 hours per week × 45 weeks × $133.33 per hour). The annual cost of an assistant working 15 hours per week, 48 weeks a year, at $25 an hour is $18,000. Your return on investment is approximately 5 to 1. If you then spend those freed-up 15 hours per week doing $133.33-an-hour work, that's an additional $90,000 in revenue.

With this exercise, you've calculated the ROI of a new assistant and written their job description. Now, go hire them. You might only need someone for ten hours a week, or thirty hours, or you might need them full time. But that person is out there waiting to take those burdens off you. Because that is what gives *them* energy.

We will now try to drive this Discipline home with this impactful analogy. Let's pretend you are a gifted surgeon. You are so specialized in your gift that only you can perform your lifesaving surgery. You love doing it, and every time you do it, you make $1,000. You are able to perform this surgery in thirty minutes, and it saves a life every time.

This surgery requires you to be energized, rested, and alert. To stay that way, you can only work forty weeks a year and forty hours per week. If you do any more, you burn out, start making mistakes, and kill patients.

The quick math is that you would save 3,200 lives per year if you put all of your working time (your work container, or your 100%) into performing your lifesaving surgery.

The only drawback is that you have to spend ten hours per week booking your travel, checking your mail and email, and other administrative tasks. So do you pay someone $25 an hour to do your administrative work, or do it yourself and let twenty people die per week?

Okay, you are not that surgeon, but you do have a super-power unique to you. What is it? If you spend all of your working time doing it and delegating all else, you will make a much bigger impact.

CHAPTER SUMMARY

The Point

Never do anything you could pay someone $25 an hour to do.

Three Thought Prompts

1. Do you check your email while in bed?
2. If you had fifteen more hours per week, what would you do with it? Spend three to five minutes writing down your answer.
3. Write down three reasons you believe you should *not* hire an assistant. Confront that fear. Then shed it by reading each answer and writing down why you feel that way about each.

_____

_____

_____

_____

_____

_____

_____

_____

_____

_____

_____

_____

_____

_____

_____

_____

_____

_____

_____

_____

_____

_____

_____

_____

_____

_____

_____

_____

_____

_____

_____

_____

_____

_____

PREPARE EVERY NIGHT

The point of this Discipline is:

Before your head hits the pillow every night,
document the next day's plan.

This is the shortest chapter of The 10 Disciplines, but don't let its length fool you into thinking it's less impactful.

I've been practicing this Discipline for twenty-five years. You should go to bed knowing exactly what you're going to do tomorrow. To make a bigger impact, you have to hit the ground running when you wake up.

Every night before I go to bed, I lay out my entire next day on a legal pad. I use a legal pad because I believe in the power of writing by hand, but you can use a tablet, a journal, your calendar, or a laptop. I time-block everything I need to do: the calls I need to make, the meetings I need to attend, the projects I need to finish. I list them all in chronological order so that the next day is charted.

Rob does the same thing. He spends twenty minutes at the end of each day writing out the next day's schedule on his tablet and determining the top three most impactful things he will do that day.

Although optional, adding the three most impactful things can be powerful. Those things might be as simple as being fully present with your loved ones or team members. Or it might be to close a deal you have been working on. With an intention in place, you have a greater likelihood of accomplishing it by expressing that positive energy in words.

Why do it the evening before? You will sleep better. You will wake up with ideas and have more creative answers to problems and projects you need to work on the next day. That's because your subconscious will be working on them while you sleep.

Let's say you are the kind of person who doesn't plan your days. You say, "I like to be spontaneous and let the day come at me," or "I like to check my emails first and see what's in store for me today," or "I just react to the calls and problems that arrive throughout the day." The sad fact is, you have lost control of your life. You're letting other people manage your energy and time.

This Discipline, Prepare Every Night, and the next one, Put Everything in One Place, are so simple and powerful that when we teach them to our clients, they are often in disbelief that they were not taught this earlier in their careers. They quickly see how this Discipline greatly increases their energy, clarity, productivity, confidence, impact, and peace.

Please commit to carrying out this practice for an entire week before you come to any conclusion. We get such great feedback when people first try this Discipline. You'll see right away how much it helps.

As we've mentioned, all of the Disciplines are interconnected and strongest when brought together. One thing we would encourage you to bring into this Discipline is to See It Every Night. I encourage you to think of the most important thing from your 10-Year Thinking Vision and see it clearly before your head hits the pillow. As Earl Nightingale teaches in his recording, "The Strangest Secret," "We become what we think about."

By preparing the night before, you will achieve the peace and space that will let your mind expand to your new possibilities the next day.

CHAPTER SUMMARY

The Point

Before your head hits the pillow every night, document the next day's plan.

Three Thought Prompts

1. How do you Prepare Every Night?
2. Reflect on a time when you felt completely *unprepared* for the next day. What sensations did you feel in your body? What emotions came up for you? How did the day go?
3. Reflect on a time when you felt completely *prepared* for the next day. What sensations did you feel in your body? What emotions came up for you? How did the day go?

_____

_____

_____

_____

_____

_____

_____

_____

_____

_____

PUT EVERYTHING IN ONE PLACE

The main point of this Discipline is:

*Pick the one place where you will capture every idea,
commitment, thought, action item, and promise.*

Let's take one aspect from the last Discipline a step further.
I've been working from a legal pad for thirty years. My clients,
friends, and peers lovingly laugh at my legal pad because it seems
so archaic. It's always with me: when I walk into any meeting,
every session, when I'm on a call, when I'm driving. I live from a
legal pad. This is my One Place.

You can also execute this Discipline on a smartphone, tablet, or laptop. It has occurred to me that if I used a tablet, many
people would probably take me more seriously. I recommend
paper or a device you can write (instead of type) on. As I've

mentioned, I believe that when you write things down, you retain them better.

Here's the typical day of an entrepreneur. Let's assume you started working from the list you laid out the night before. As you work through the day, you have meetings and phone calls, you get ideas, you make promises to people, emotions and thoughts come up, and you have to remember numerous work items. Normally, you put each of these items somewhere, maybe on a sticky note, and set it aside. You might try to juggle all of them in your head. Or you might tap them into your phone or text them to yourself. Yet by the end of the day, you have compiled a messy grab bag of stuff you're supposed to do. And the truth is, you've probably forgotten some of it. Your brain can't keep track of all of that stuff. As a result, you're probably dropping some balls and letting people down.

At this point, I'm sure we don't have to tell you what that is doing to your energy, impact, or level of peace. I'm guessing you lost a little energy just reading that paragraph.

After learning this Discipline, a client shared a painful discovery. He surveyed his desk, which had sticky notes all over the place. Some were days old, while others were months old. Inspired by the session, he was determined to clean up his desk, free himself from sticky notes, and pick his One Place. As he went through each note, he found one, buried under some papers, that turned out to be important. He had needed to follow up on a very large and potentially lucrative deal. Because the sticky note got buried for months, he forgot all about it and lost out on the deal. He felt sick to his stomach and vowed he would never let that happen again. Now, using his One Place, he has a greater peace of mind and feels more in control. This example is a perfect illustration of what likely is happening to you when you have no process for grouping all your notes in One Place.

On my ever-present legal pad, I write down any promises I make to others, ideas, anything I need to remember, tasks to follow up on, or a download—which is an inspiration, something my intuition is telling me, or my mind bringing me ideas. Every evening when I prepare for the next day, I can pull all of those commitments, thoughts, and ideas off the pad and assign them in their appropriate spot in my planning. I might put some on the list for the next day, or take care of an item right then and there at night while I'm preparing. Some I compartmentalize as to-dos in my calendar or time-block them as a future project.

This process will also help you heighten and cultivate your awareness. You may have made an important decision, then had a feeling or thought come up. You can jot it down to process later. While reviewing your notes on your One Place at the end of the day, you can think about whether you made the decision out of love or fear or if the thought or feeling was love based or fear based. Or, while walking into a client meeting, you might notice a strong feeling appear in your body. Use your One Place to write down what is happening. During your Be Still time the next day, you can explore what was going on. Why did that meeting, for example, provoke an off feeling? Then you can work to unblock your energy.

By not having One Place, you are holding yourself back from making a greater impact in the world. With your One Place, you will be less stressed because everything that is usually rolling around in your mind is now safely stored away. Less stress is freedom. Freedom allows you time to stay aware and better Know Thyself, which cultivates intuition, creativity, and ideas.

Please try this tomorrow. Decide the One Place you're going to put every single workday commitment, idea, and thought. Then capture everything that comes up throughout the day in that place. Try it for a week and see how it affects your productivity and energy.

CHAPTER SUMMARY

The Point

Pick the One Place where you will capture every idea, commitment, thought, action item, and promise.

Three Thought Prompts

1. Write down all the ways you currently capture all information throughout the day. What works and what doesn't?

2. Reflect on a time you let a team member / employee or loved one down because your system for organizing tasks failed you. What happened? When you think about this, what sensations do you feel in your body?

3. Review your 10-Year Thinking Vision. How does each one of the commitments, ideas, and thoughts that come up daily align with what you see for your life in the future?

_____

_____

_____

_____

_____

_____

_____

_____

BE HUMBLE

The main point of this Discipline is:

View yourself as an equal to every person on the planet.

What does being humble have to do with impact and peace? Everything. Let me explain. First of all, I'm not talking about being weak. Humble people are powerful and strong. Pastor and author Rick Warren said, "Humility is not thinking less of yourself, it is thinking of yourself less."

What does being humble have to do with becoming your True Self? Everything. When you are your True Self, you realize that everything and everyone is connected. You realize that you don't have to prove anything to anyone. You just want to be yourself. You understand that living from the outside in does not work anymore and that living from the inside out makes for a better life. Your True Self guides how you show up in the world by providing genuine care in every one of your actions and interactions.

Start by picturing a spectrum. On one end is "arrogant." On the other is "humble."

Arrogant  Humble

I'm guessing you know both types of people. The definition of "humble" is, ironically, similar to the definition of "arrogant." "Humble" means "your estimate of your own importance in comparison to others," and "arrogant" means "the way you view your level of importance in comparison to others." They are both saying the same thing, but the difference lies in how much more important than others a person feels they are. Humble people don't feel they are more important than anyone else. Arrogant people feel that they are.

What is your view of yourself? To see how you stack up, draw the above spectrum, and then put a hash mark where you feel you are on it. If you want a more accurate depiction, ask five people closest to you where they would put you on the spectrum.

Peace comes when we stop making it about us. When we feel whole and complete, it is no longer about us, it's about others. When you shift the focus from you to them, that's when you start making a bigger impact.

Whether you are arrogant or humble, you can be extremely successful, of course. There are thousands of examples of both types of people. What I have discovered, however, is that the journey of life is better if you are humble. There is a universal law—the boomerang, karma, whatever you call it—that being humble in life attracts more humble people to you, which leads to more happiness, friends, and people who want to be with you and love you unconditionally. It's the same thing I shared about high- and low-vibration energy attracting the same energy. Like attracts like.

I am grateful to my father-in-law, Neil Pardun, for teaching me humility. When I was in my twenties, I was going down a path of arrogance. He altered the course of my life by his example. He didn't even know he did it. He didn't pull me aside and say, "Hey, be more humble." He showed it through the example of his actions.

Neil was a wealthy man who made his money constructing industrial buildings and also owned a golf course. He was a tough guy, down to earth, authentic, and generous. He was always fully himself and didn't care what anyone thought. He treated everyone the same and always made you feel important. Everyone liked and respected him.

I have two favorite stories about Neil. Once, while I was driving him home, he saw a set of ratty, dusty old golf clubs in someone's trash on garbage day. He yelled, "Stop the car!" He jumped out and garbage-picked the tattered old clubs because they could be used at his golf course. It was not beneath him to pick someone's trash if he thought it had utility.

The second story happened while he was working at the golf course. He would cut the greens every day while wearing his old jeans and a T-shirt. One day some young kids were horsing around on the course while he was on his mower. He rode over and asked them to stop. They asked, "Who do you think you are, old man?"

Neil said, "I'm the owner."

One of the kids said, "Yeah, right!" Neil just laughed and rode away.

You'd never guess he had money. I'm thankful every day that Neil was in my life.

Check Yourself

Some of our clients rank themselves on the high end of humble, which does not surprise me, as humble people are drawn to this work. That said, we challenge them during this exercise to ponder the following three scenarios, as being humble can be subtle.

- Have you ever been at a restaurant, feeling "hangry" and in a bit of a rush, and found the service not up to your expectations? In that scenario, maybe you treated the server with a slight edge. Maybe when the server was away from your table, you shook your head and made a judgment about this person.
- Have you ever arrived at a hotel or resort where the staff took care of your every whim? How did that make you feel? Again, did you feel more important than members of the staff, or did you feel like a complete equal?
- Have you ever been in a meeting with employees and, while discussing an issue, felt frustrated that they weren't at the same level as you were?

Beyond these scenarios, maybe one time you came home from a busy and challenging day and shared with a significant other about a drama at work. Reflecting on that time, were you the person who was "right" in the scenario? What part did your ego play in your description of the events that took place? Were you frustrated about the person who was part of the situation? Was there a subtle sense that you were smarter, even better?

In terms of energy management, when you are humble, you get more energy back from people than you put out. You are therefore having an impact. You also attract more people who mirror your attitude. Do you want to be surrounded by humble people or arrogant people?

When you are humble, you come from love and not from fear. When you come from fear, your unresolved pain, trauma, and wounds are blocking you, and your ego can cause you to become arrogant. And that arrogance will attract other arrogant people.

As Joe Stewart, an EOS Implementer, says, "You can't shed your shit if you think you're the shit."

When you are coming from love, you have self-trust, presence, flow, and awareness. Your intuition is stronger, you feel connected, you naturally let go, and your energy is vibrating high. You can just be. This is humility.

Being humble and being grateful go hand in hand. While creating The 10 Disciplines, I wondered if Discipline 10 should be "Be Humble" or "Be Grateful." Then I realized that I've never met a humble person who did not feel gratitude daily. I decided to use "Be Humble," knowing that gratitude is a component of it.

In his book *How to Be Well: The 6 Keys to a Happy and Healthy Life*, Frank Lipman, MD, writes, "Gratitude is turning your attention to the goodness that is already in your life. When you view your world through a thankful lens, more good things start to happen. It's a simple but powerful way to reframe your perspective on life."

Here's a simple practice. Say "Thank you" every night when you go to bed. You can piggyback that on your visualization, Seeing It Every Night, as we discussed earlier.

CHAPTER SUMMARY

The Point

View yourself as an equal to every person on the planet.

Three Thought Prompts

1. Rate yourself on the Arrogant to Humble scale. Then ask the five people closest to you to rank you on the Arrogant to Humble scale. This will help you determine how the world sees you.

2. Write down the name of a person in your life who is the perfect example of humility. List three to five traits this person has. Regard this person as a role model of humility to guide your actions in life.

3. List the ten people closest to you and rate each of them on the Arrogant to Humble scale. This will help you understand who you are attracting.

_____

_____

_____

_____

_____

_____

_____

The 10 Disciplines—Summary

The foundation of The 10 Disciplines creates freedom in your life, which opens up space in your mind and time in your life to do the outer and inner world work. By doing so, you will become your True Self.

Each discipline is simple. Doing them is harder. Please don't underestimate them, as they will have a profound impact on your life. If you implement every one of these disciplines, you will be a force of nature.

Here are The 10 Disciplines for Maximizing Your Impact and Inner Peace at a glance, along with the main point of each:

1. **10-Year Thinking**

   Shift your mind from short-term thinking to thinking in ten-year time frames.

2. **Take Time Off**

   Take 130 days off per year and don't think about work the entire day.

3. **Know Thyself**

   Be your True Self 100% of the time, 24/7/365.

4. **Be Still**

   Sit in silence for thirty minutes every day.

5. **Know Your 100%**

   Decide on and commit to the perfect number of hours per week and weeks per year that you will deliver your impact to the world.

6. **Say No ... Often**

   Say no to everything that doesn't fit into the first five Disciplines.

7. **Don't Do $25-an-Hour Work**

   Never do anything you could pay someone $25 an hour to do.

8. **Prepare Every Night**

   Before your head hits the pillow every night, document the next day's plan.

9. **Put Everything in One Place**

   Pick the one place you will capture every idea, commitment, thought, action item, and promise.

10. **Be Humble**

    View yourself as an equal to every person on the planet.

Go to The10Disciplines.com/book and download the following visual to keep on your computer, desk, or smartphone, both as a daily reminder of each one and to see how they are interconnected.

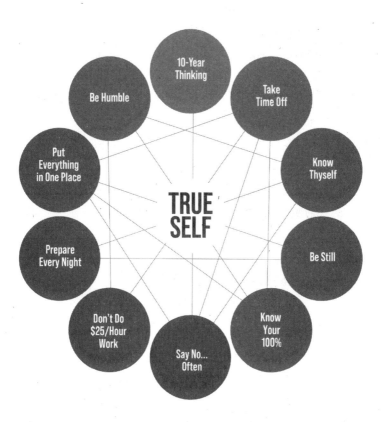

BEING YOUR TRUE SELF—SHINE

So there it is. How to free your True Self, have a bigger impact, and enjoy inner peace.

The first half of this book showed what you can achieve with The 3 Discoveries: the possibility of managing your driven DNA, shedding all your layers to become your True Self, and realizing that it is possible to be driven *and* have peace.

The second half of this book showed you how to do it: by implementing The 10 Disciplines, which ultimately will help you maximize the impact you have on the world and enjoy peace while doing it.

We truly hope you will join us on this journey. But if you're not ready, that's okay. If you are not called to this, that's okay too. If you had to muscle your way through every word because you feel you have to or someone is pressuring you, this may not be the right time for you. Maybe focusing on outer world success is what you should do right now.

If you want to keep growing, though—go deeper, become the best version of yourself—you now have a road map. There's nothing you have to do right now but want it. Our goal with this book is to tap you on the shoulder, pierce the layers of your armor, and let a little light in . . . or a little light out.

I've been asked: Is this religion, spirituality, or science? Who knows? Whatever it is called, the beauty is that it is timeless and universal. You get to bring whatever your experience has been. It all fits. We are all just human beings trying to create something meaningful in this world.

I don't know if I'm 1 percent or 100 percent of the way to freeing my True Self. It's a journey. I realize that every day is different. Some days I feel like I'm at 10 percent, and others 80 percent. It's like drilling for oil.

Every time I reach a new level of growth, something profound happens that shows me the endless possibilities. There is more work to do, and it keeps getting better.

Rob likes to say, there is no scorecard for this. What are you keeping score of? Your True Self is innate within you, and it can, and likely does, come out every day. With the tools we've written about, you have the opportunity to be your True Self more often than not.

If this book resonated with you, then please trust that you are in the right place. The work might be challenging, but it will be incredibly rewarding, the most rewarding work you will ever do. We also urge you to read this book multiple times, as each time you will be in a different mind frame and have new "aha!"s.

Now, let's talk about what is really possible. Picture yourself as a radiant ball of pure energy, shining bright, with no blocks, restrictions, or distortions. Energy flows freely through you. Top to bottom, side to side. It is clean, clear, and light. You're vibrating at the highest level. Attracting to yourself everything that you desire. Your intuition is fully online, and you are making your decisions from love. When issues, problems, and emotions arise, you process them and solve them, and they freely flow through you without getting stuck or triggering you.

As we noted while discussing Discovery #1, a driven entrepreneur touches an average of about two hundred people in their life. Our mission is to impact one million driven entrepreneurs, helping them become their True Selves. Assuming we achieve our goal, and you are touching two hundred people in your life, that's *two hundred million* people whom this message will impact.

If you do this work, the people in your life are going to notice a change in you. When they ask what's going on, please teach it to them. Don't teach it before they ask, though. You have to be the example first. As my dad says, "The best way for people to not take your advice is for you to offer it to them." When the student is ready, the teacher appears. Teaching them will be the greatest reward for your achieving this balance. It is like building a bridge so others can cross it.

Imagine everyone vibrating high on this planet, being impactful and peaceful. Serving the way they are called to serve, whether that's building a company, flipping a hamburger, or helping a loved one. As long as they're being their True Self, there is no bad option. The True Self Model applies to everyone.

THE TRUE SELF MODEL

BALANCE

IMPACT   PEACE

INSECURITY   WORK   SELF-TRUST   FEAR
FEAR   CREATE PRODUCE   LOVE INTUITION BE   PAIN
FAILURE   CRAFT MANIFEST EARN   PRESENCE FLOW ENERGY   TRAUMA
DOUBT   DO VALUE SERVE   CONNECTED LET GO   WOUNDING
LACK OF   DRIVE   AWARENESS   EGO
CONFIDENCE

OUTER WORLD   INNER WORLD

TRUE SELF
FREEDOM, CREATIVITY, & IMPACT
LET YOUR FREAK FLAG FLY
FLOWT

Then, imagine each of these people being peaceful, with no blocked energy, no trauma, no pain, no baggage, no ego, no fear. Operating from the inside out. Making love-based decisions.

If we lived in this state, words wouldn't matter. No one would be offended or have their feelings hurt. Because we would know that what someone else says is their choice and know that their words have nothing to do with us. So why would we take that personally? You only get triggered by words because of an issue going on inside you.

Words don't matter if they're coming from love and being received by love. And if they are coming from fear, hate, and ego, they won't affect you because you are free from your ego.

When you react to what someone says, they control you. It is certainly okay to respond, but know that when you do, your response is your words, your opinion, and hopefully from love.

If you still feel like you are climbing a mountain, we hope you soon realize . . . there is no mountain. The whole process is a journey, on which you're making a bigger and bigger impact while enjoying more and more inner peace, continually growing, and just experiencing life.

Experiencing life, in addition to being your True Self and Flowting through life, also means that you will still have setbacks, have to deal with difficult people, have bad days, and vibrate low sometimes.

I am a driven entrepreneur like you. I spend forty weeks a year and fifty hours a week Flowting through the five pieces of content that I created (the four listed at the beginning of this book, plus this book). I do this by delivering speeches, sessions, podcasts, and writing. And in this wonderful state, I'm still able to make very tough business decisions, have very difficult conversations with employees, and deal with many very dramatic people, all while writing this book. In fact, in the last eighteen months, I wrote this book and started two new businesses! I can't stop myself from making an impact.

Yet, life still goes on. I interact with many people, and most of them are in pain. Heck, I'm still shedding my pain from early in my life. I also lost my fifty-eight-year-old brother while writing this book. He died suddenly from a massive heart attack. He was my hero and my rock. I believe the shedding I've done and the peace I am now experiencing have greatly helped me grieve and process his death in a very healthy way. I fear for how I might have handled it prior to my awakening. Yet despite my own pain and that of the people I meet, I still have to interact with them. I still have to be a businessman. I still have to live a life, be a family man and friend. But all of those interactions are so much more peaceful now. I can stay calm in the storm.

When I'm with an audience of driven entrepreneurs, I start by saying, "We are the same." I truly believe this. We driven entrepreneurs are all the same balls of energy inside. The only thing different is our story and our packaging. We all look different and took a different path to get here, yet our True Selves are the same.

We are here to make an impact. It is what we are built to do. We want to grow, build, create, work, be productive. We can't stop ourselves. That's the driven DNA.

While I have shed a lot of my stuff, I still have more to shed. I am writing this book while still in the game, not after having won it. I'm just sharing my experience in real time—in the hopes that it will help all of us.

On that note, I had a funny experience this week. We had received all of our test-reader feedback on this book, which was incredible, and I was overwhelmed because I didn't think we could get through all the writing and make the editing changes in time for our publishing deadline.

I woke up feeling the old pressure and intensity that used to drive me and thought, "Man, I hope I can get through this and get back to living." And then the truth hit me: this is living. It is all living. There was nothing to get "through." An incredible peace came over me, I got to work, and the words I needed flowed like water.

I had five days to finalize my part of the test-reader feedback, and I'm going to make it with about fifteen minutes to spare. Crazy!

It makes me think of all the times I stressed myself out trying to get "through" something, and the times I might do the same in the future. It's all just life. I'm going to relax, let go, and experience it. I hope that means something to you.

So, after finding your True Self, you will still grow your company, fend off competitors, fire people, have conflicts, and make very tough decisions. But you will do it from love and with inner peace.

You will be more *you* than ever. The change will probably be subtle for the people around you, but you will feel a state of bliss and fulfillment inside like never before.

If every one of us got there, oh, what a world it would be.

Please take a minute right now and take the True Self Assessment again to see if you've made progress since taking it at the beginning of this book. This will also set your baseline as you now begin implementing The 10 Disciplines. We urge you to take the assessment quarterly and keep measuring your progress toward becoming your True Self. You can also take it at The10Disciplines.com/book. Also, please send the link to a driven entrepreneur you know who would benefit from taking the assessment.

THE TRUE SELF ASSESSMENT

Read each of the following statements and rank yourself 1–5, where 1 is "not true" and 5 is "100% true."

		1	2	3	4	5
1.	In all of my decisions, thoughts, and actions, I have at least a ten-year time frame in mind.	❏	❏	❏	❏	❏
2.	I spend enough time away from work to rest and reset my energy and clarity levels.	❏	❏	❏	❏	❏
3.	I am comfortable and confident being my True Self in every personal and professional situation.	❏	❏	❏	❏	❏
4.	I consistently practice stillness to create space and clarity in my life.	❏	❏	❏	❏	❏
5.	I know the perfect amount of hours per day and weeks per year during which I want to deliver my value to the world.	❏	❏	❏	❏	❏
6.	I know when to say no, to say no often, and to set effective boundaries.	❏	❏	❏	❏	❏
7.	I know my superpower and delegate all the work that competes with my productivity and drains my energy.	❏	❏	❏	❏	❏
8.	I end every day with a plan in place for tomorrow.	❏	❏	❏	❏	❏
9.	I am organized, consistent, and never drop the ball on promises or commitments made to others.	❏	❏	❏	❏	❏
10.	I practice empathy toward, view myself as equal to, and respect everyone I encounter.	❏	❏	❏	❏	❏

11. I have worked through all past trauma and left behind all feelings of anxiety, shame, or depression. ❏ ❏ ❏ ❏ ❏

12. I am aware of the ways my drive is a blessing and a curse. ❏ ❏ ❏ ❏ ❏

13. I completely understand that I am made up of pure energy and know when my energy is blocked. ❏ ❏ ❏ ❏ ❏

14. I am aware of my pain/trauma and can remove the associated blocked energy preventing me from experiencing peace. ❏ ❏ ❏ ❏ ❏

15. I am aware of and connected to my True Self. ❏ ❏ ❏ ❏ ❏

16. I know when I am making decisions out of love or fear. ❏ ❏ ❏ ❏ ❏

17. I am fully present, aware, and connected to the people around me at every moment. ❏ ❏ ❏ ❏ ❏

18. I am making the impact I want in the world. ❏ ❏ ❏ ❏ ❏

19. I feel a sense of peace, joy, fulfillment, and bliss in my life. ❏ ❏ ❏ ❏ ❏

20. I am completely free to be my True Self always. ❏ ❏ ❏ ❏ ❏

Total number of each ranking	❏	❏	❏	❏	❏
	x1	x2	x3	x4	x5
Multiply by the number above	❏	❏	❏	❏	❏

Add all five numbers to determine the percentage score that reflects you being your True Self.

_____%

As you review your results a second time, we invite you to reflect on the five most important things you are taking away from this book and the next steps you will take to free your True Self. Write your thoughts in the space below:

_____

_____

_____

_____

_____

_____

_____

_____

_____

_____

Now, let's go to work!

Rob and I hope you will continue this important work once you set this book down. But please pick the book up again regularly and use it as a reference point in order to reinforce the ideas often. At The10Disciplines.com/book, in addition to the True Self Assessment, you will find free resources such as our weekly blog. If you are interested in deepening this work, we list our offerings, and resources for shedding layers hereafter.

We wish you all the best in freeing your True Self. Stay focused and much love!

The 10 Disciplines Offerings

If you've come this far, you may feel inspired to implement The 10 Disciplines on your own.

You may also be wondering how to get extra support in that journey.

Please go to The10Disciplines.com/book to discover all of the resources we have available for you. In addition to the graphics and resources described in the book, you'll also find:

- **Weekly Blog:** Each week you'll receive a Discovery from Gino or Rob to direct you further in your True Self Journey.
- **The True Self Assessment:** Take our free assessment quarterly to gauge where you are on your True Self journey, and how much more of yourself can be freed.
- **The 10 Disciplines-Specific Programs:** If you want to explore The 10 Disciplines even further, we have programs created to help you implement each Discipline into your life and business.
- **Self-Study Journey:** Gino Wickman guides you through our self-study video course using in-depth teachings and interactive experiences for each of The 10 Disciplines. Work through the course at your own pace to learn and successfully implement The 10 Disciplines into your life.
- **Group Coaching Program:** Our live coaching program guides you through the Disciplines to ensure you master each, and intertwine them for maximum impact. Fast-paced, experiential working sessions will promote interaction and

connection with your fellow 10 Disciplines members. We strongly believe that the support of this community will help you layer these learnings into your life more effortlessly. Choose to become a VIP and dive even deeper with 1:1 sessions with a personal 10 Disciplines coach.

- **True Self Mastermind:** Once you have a strong foundation in place and graduate from The 10 Disciplines Self-Study Journey or Group Coaching Program, you are invited to join Gino and Rob live on the journey in the True Self Mastermind. These sessions take a deeper dive into The 3 Discoveries and 10 Disciplines and offer access to new content Gino and Rob are learning about and creating. Here, remarkable people gather to learn, share experiences, and shed layers to help one another free their True Selves.

If you would like to join us in any of these resources and opportunities, find more information at The10Disciplines.com /book.

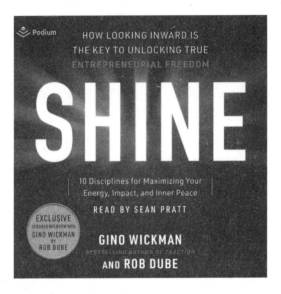

RESOURCES FOR SHEDDING LAYERS

In this section, we share resources, books, and experts on shedding layers from our own personal experiences as well as those that contributed to this book. We are not experts or professionals in any of these areas; they are not recommendations but rather a guide to help you begin your own investigation.

Also, remember that you don't have to do any of these. As we've shared, you can shed layers on your own through stillness, awareness, and releasing what comes up.

Still, we encourage you to read through the list and notice if any jump out at you. When you are ready, a resource from this list may pique your interest and draw you in to learn more. In some cases, we will provide specific contact information; most of the resources will require more investigation on your part. Of course, you can find many resources beyond those listed here, and we also encourage you to seek those out.

Acupuncture: A traditional Chinese medicine practice that involves inserting thin needles into specific points on the body to stimulate energy flow. It can help ease pain, lower stress, improve sleep, and increase overall wellness by inducing the body to heal on its own.

Akashic Reading: A spiritual practice that involves accessing the Akashic Records, often described as a cosmic database of every word, thought, and action that has ever occurred. It can provide individuals with profound insights into their past, present, and potential future, thereby promoting personal growth and spiritual development.

Astrology: A study and belief system suggesting there is a relationship between the positions of the celestial bodies (planets and stars) and events that occur on Earth. It is often used as a tool for understanding oneself, predicting future trends, and making decisions in various aspects of life.

Books:

- *The Untethered Soul: The Journey Beyond Yourself* by Michael Singer: Walks you through your thoughts and emotions, helping you to uncover the source and fluctuations of your inner energy and delving into what you can do to free yourself from your habitual thoughts, emotions, and energy patterns that limit your consciousness, opening the door to a life lived in the freedom of your innermost being.
- *Letting Go: The Pathway of Surrender* by David Hawkins: A practical technique by which to remove inner blocks to happiness, love, joy, success, health, and ultimately,

Enlightenment. The book provides the mechanism for letting go of those blocks in the midst of everyday life.

- *Driven: Understanding and Harnessing the Genetic Gifts Shared by Entrepreneurs, Navy SEALs, Pro Athletes, and Maybe YOU* by Douglas Brackmann, PhD: Some people are born with a drive often seen in entrepreneurs, pro athletes, inventors, adventurers, and Navy SEALs. It's in their DNA; research has shown that certain genes can manifest resilient and highly focused people who can also be impulsive and easily distracted. This book teaches you how to use this gift.

- *Why Woo-Woo Works: The Surprising Science Behind Meditation, Reiki, Crystals, and Other Alternative Practices* by David Hamilton: Alternative therapies, healing modalities, and spiritual practices are often referred to as "woo-woo," but many of these approaches are actually supported by compelling scientific evidence.

- *The Wise Heart: A Guide to the Universal Teachings of Buddhist Psychology* by Jack Kornfield: A book about awakening your capability for extraordinary love, for joy, for communion with life, and unshakable freedom.

Breathwork: The practice of conscious and controlled breathing techniques that can be useful in reducing stress, promoting relaxation, and enhancing self-awareness.

- Pranayama: A yoga-based practice involving controlled breathing techniques to enhance the flow of energy in the body.

- Holotropic: A practice that involves rapid, deep breathing to induce altered states of consciousness for psychological and spiritual growth.
- Transformational: A practice of full, connected breathing (inhale and exhale with no pause) to release tension and promote physical and emotional well-being.
- Box/Four Square: A practice that involves inhaling, holding the breath for four seconds, exhaling, and holding the breath again for the same count. The purpose is to reduce stress and improve concentration.
- Wim Hof Method: A practice that combines specific breathing patterns with cold exposure and meditation to increase resilience, energy, and well-being.

Contemplation: A form of mindful introspection where you focus on a specific idea or topic. It allows for deeper understanding and clarity of thought and can promote personal growth and emotional regulation. Examples are time in nature, reflective writing, and deep listening.

Energy Healing: A holistic practice to activate the body's subtle energy systems to remove blocks and stimulate its ability to heal itself. It is used to reduce stress and anxiety and promote well-being.

Journaling: The practice of regularly writing down your thoughts, feelings, and experiences. It can be beneficial to help clarify thoughts, process emotions, enhance self-awareness, reduce stress, express gratitude, and improve mental health.

- Reflective Journaling: Writing about your day, your inter-actions, and your thoughts to gain insight and clarity.
- Gratitude Journaling: Listing things you are grateful for, which promotes positivity and more clarity in your life.
- Dream Journaling: Writing down dreams upon wak-ing to help understand your subconscious thoughts and patterns.
- Art Journaling: Using images, colors, and collages as well as words to express your thoughts and feelings as well as enhance your creativity and self-expression.

Meditation: The practice of training the mind to focus and redirect thoughts to promote mental clarity and emotional calm.

Types:
- Centering Prayer Meditation: A form of contempla-tive prayer involving choosing a sacred word or a symbol of your intention to consent to God's presence and action within. It involves sitting in silence, letting go of thoughts, and focusing on the word or symbol to bring the mind back to stillness and openness to the divine.
- Loving-Kindness Meditation: Focusing on developing feelings of compassion and love for oneself and others.
- Mindfulness Meditation: Focusing on the present moment and accepting it without judgment.
- Transcendental Meditation: Silently repeating a mantra to facilitate a state of relaxed awareness.

Books on Meditation:

- *10% Happier: How I Tamed the Voice in My Head, Reduced Stress Without Losing My Edge, and Found Self-Help That Actually Works—A True Story* by Dan Harris: Former *Nightline* anchor Dan Harris embarks on an unexpected, hilarious, and deeply skeptical odyssey through the strange worlds of spirituality and self-help, and discovers a way to get happier that is truly achievable.

- *The Mindful Athlete: Secrets to Pure Performance* by George Mumford: Michael Jordan, Kobe Bryant, and countless other NBA players turned around their games because of George Mumford's transformative teaching. Mumford shares his own story and the strategies that have made these athletes into stars through his proven, gentle, but groundbreaking mindfulness techniques that can transform anyone with a goal.

- *Meditation for Beginners* by Jack Kornfield, PhD: Trusted teacher Jack Kornfield shows you how simple it is to start—and stick with—a daily meditation practice.

Courses:

- Sounds True, soundstrue.com
- The Mindful Athlete Course by George Mumford, georgemumford.com
- Transcendental Meditation, tm.org
- Tara Brach Radical Compassion Institute, tarabrach.com

Prayer: A spiritual practice often found in religious and spiritual traditions. During prayer, individuals communicate with a higher power or their own inner wisdom, seeking guidance, expressing gratitude, or asking for assistance. It can provide comfort during challenging times; foster a sense of connection with something larger than oneself; serve as a reflection on one's thoughts and feelings; and cultivate gratitude, humility, and patience. It can also reduce stress and improve mental health.

Psychedelics/Plant Medicine: Substances derived from certain plants and fungi such as psilocybin mushrooms, ayahuasca, and peyote, which induce altered states of consciousness, perceptions, and emotions. *Under safe, clinical, and guided use*, along with integration, the therapeutic effects can include reduced symptoms of depression, anxiety, posttraumatic stress disorder, and addiction, as well as personal and spiritual growth, increased creativity, and a greater sense of connectedness or unity.

Red Light Therapy: Therapy designed to use the power of light at a certain wavelength to stimulate the healing power of the body.

Reiki Therapy: Energy healing from a reiki master who uses gentle hand movements with the intention of guiding the flow of healthy energy through the body.

Retreats: Dedicated time and space away from your daily activities and stressors to focus on personal growth, spiritual development, deepening faith, relaxation, and rejuvenation. Benefits can include improved mental and physical health, deeper self-awareness, inspiration, and fostering a sense of connection with like-minded individuals.

Tell Your Inner Story: As we shared earlier, there is power in telling your inner story. Doing this with people close to you can help you process and heal from the experience and strengthen your bond through vulnerability and trust.

The Process One Exercise: A way to help you process blocked energy, shared earlier in the book in Discovery #2, The Blocked Energy Level: You Can Remove Blocked Energy.

Therapy: Often referred to as psychotherapy or counseling, this is a process of working with a trained professional to explore behaviors, beliefs, feelings, relationship issues, or significant life changes. Therapy can provide strategies to manage symptoms, cope with challenges, improve mental health and wellness, increase self-understanding, and enhance quality of life.

Types:

- Cognitive-behavioral therapy: A form of talk therapy to help you manage your problems by changing how you think and behave.
- Dialectical behavior therapy: A structured program of psychotherapy with a strong educational component designed to provide skills for managing intense emotions and negotiating social relationships.[*]
- Psychodynamic therapy: Focuses on the roots of emotional suffering through self-reflection and self-examination.

---

[*] From *Psychology Today*, www.psychologytoday.com/us/therapy-types /dialectical-behavior-therapy.

- Humanistic therapy: This form of talk therapy focuses on a person's individual nature, focusing on the whole person, their positive characteristics, and potential for growth.*
- Mindfulness-based therapy: A modified form of cognitive therapy incorporating mindfulness practices such as present moment awareness, meditation, and breathing exercises.†
- Family therapy: This form of talk therapy focuses on improving interfamilial relationships and behaviors.
- Group therapy: A form of therapy that involves one or more psychologists who lead a group of approximately five to fifteen patients to help them help themselves and others, often targeting a specific problem.
- Eye movement desensitization and reprocessing: A structured therapy that encourages the patient to briefly focus on a memory of trauma while simultaneously experiencing bilateral stimulation (eye movements), which is associated with a reduction in the strength of emotions associated with the memories.
- Art therapy: Patients use art to interpret, express, and resolve their emotions and thoughts.
- Psychedelic-assisted therapy: This practice incorporates psychedelics to help facilitate deep personal insight and healing.

---

* From *Psychology Today*, www.psychologytoday.com/us/therapy-types /humanistic-therapy.

† From Castle Craig, www.castlecraig.co.uk/admissions/frequently-asked -questions/what-happens-in-residential-rehab/.

Resources:
- American Psychological Association, apa.org
- Psychology Today's tool for finding therapists, psychologytoday.com/us/therapists

Yoga: A physical, mental, and spiritual practice that includes postures, breath control, and meditation to bring the mind, body, and spirit together. It can improve flexibility, strength, and balance; reduce stress; and promote relaxation, self-awareness, and well-being.

Types:
- Ashtanga Yoga: Involves synchronizing the breath with a progressive series of postures: includes a process of intense internal heat and a purifying sweat that detoxifies muscles and organs.[*]
- Hatha Yoga: An old system that includes the practice of yoga postures and breathing exercises, which help bring peace to the mind and body.[†]
- Kundalini Yoga: A physical, mental, and spiritual discipline for developing strength, awareness, character, and consciousness.[‡]
- Vinyasa Yoga: Stringing postures together so that a person moves from one to the other seamlessly, using breath. It is often fast paced, vigorous, and dynamic.

---

[*] From The Yoga Shala, www.theyogashala.org/about-ashtanga-yoga.html.

[†] From DoYogaWithMe, www.doyogawithme.com/types-of-yoga.

[‡] From Lynn Roulo, www.lynnroulo.com/about/yoga/.

Other:

- The IEP (Intentional Energetic Presence) Method®: Proprietary methodology and impact model for leaders, athletes, and human beings on human performance, influence, building resiliency, cultivating trust, and creating impact. (activechoices.com)
- Danielle L. Brooks, Self-Discovery Integration and spiritual guidance: Helping people find the truth of who they are and True Self discovery. (daniellebrooks.com)
- Daniel White, Daniel White Coaching: Specializes in transforming blocks that are holding you back from living your truth. (danielwhitecoaching.com)
- Douglas Brackmann, PhD: Specializes in helping driven people end shame and self-sabotage using tools to harness your gifts. (iamdriven.com)
- Hoffman Institute: Helping people transform their lives and uncover their most powerful self. (hoffmaninstitute.org)
- *Huberman Lab*: Andrew Huberman's podcast about human performance. (hubermanlab.com)
- Power of the Breath, Art of Living: Breathing techniques and practical wisdom that can change your life. (artofliving.org/us-en/power-breath)
- The Work, Byron Katie: Meditation practice that allows you to access the wisdom that always exists within you. (thework.com)

ACKNOWLEDGMENTS

Much effort, time, and love were put into this book by many people. Rob and I were overwhelmed as we reflected on the care and support of every person who contributed to making it a success.

In this section, we would like to acknowledge our sincere appreciation to all of these people. Of course, words won't do it justice, but we will do our best.

First, thank *you*, the reader, for allowing the space in your mind and the time in your life to consider what we are teaching in this book. It's humbling.

Gino's Family, Friends, Mentors, and Teachers

Kathy, my strong, intuitive, and beautiful wife. I am so grateful for your belief and support. I appreciate and love you with all of my heart.

Alexis, my incredibly wise daughter. You are as beautiful on the inside as you are on the outside. Your conscientiousness and quiet strength makes me so proud, and you make me smile every day. I love you.

Gino, my quick-witted son. You have an engineer's mind with an incredible personality and work ethic. Thank you for always making me laugh so hard. I am so very proud of you. I love you.

Spencer Cook and Samantha Wickman, my son-in-law and daughter-in-law, you are such joyful additions to our family. I truly love the time we spend together as a family. I'm so proud of you both and love you very much.

Linda Wickman, my mom, for teaching me to be independent, for your amazing quiet strength, wisdom, and inspiration. You always make me feel so loved. I think about you every day and love you very much.

Floyd Wickman, my dad and my mentor. You are the entrepreneur's entrepreneur. You have taught me most of what I know about communicating with people, be it one or one thousand. I love you and am forever grateful.

Neil Pardun, my father-in-law, for teaching me that it is possible to possess wealth and remain humble. You've helped me keep my feet on the ground all these years. You are a rare and special person. I am forever changed through your example. I miss you greatly.

Ed Escobar, my first business partner, for pushing so hard and finally convincing my dad to let me into his company. Thanks for being so tough on me in my twenties. I now see how that transformed me. I am on this path because of your belief in me. Thank you for teaching me to never do $25-an-hour work.

Mike Pallin, who I sincerely believe is my guardian angel. You always place in front of me exactly what I need at that point in my life. You single-handedly altered the course of my life three separate times.

Karen Grooms, the world's greatest business manager. Thanks for holding all of the pieces together and protecting me from distractions for almost thirty years.

Curt Rager and Bob Shenefelt, for being an amazing sounding board and for constantly challenging me. Our annual trip to the mountains gives me tremendous clarity and insight. You are lifers.

Don Tinney, the best business partner a person could have. Thanks for fighting the good fight with me for fifteen years. We built something great together.

Sam Cupp, my business mentor, for teaching me most of what I know about business. I could not have pulled off that turnaround without your guidance. I miss you greatly since your untimely passing.

Rob Dube, my dear friend and business partner. Thank you for sticking with me during my internal storm. You ground me and make me a better person. I can't wait to see what this journey has in store for us.

To my advisers and guides, Debra Silverman, Burke Miller, Alandra Napali Kai, Daniel White, Lynn Austin, Sarah Gordon, Virgil Knyght, Danielle Brooks, and Michael Blomsterberg. Thank you all for your incredible wisdom and insight.

Joe Calhoon, Mari Tautimes, Nathen Fox, Thomas Wesner, and Laurel Romanella, for going above and beyond with your feedback, support, insight, and cheerleading during the wild evolution of this content. I really needed it.

Dan Sullivan, for helping me discover my Unique Ability® and showing me how to build a life around it. You have had a great impact on my life. You are truly the coach of all coaches.

Mr. Sarkisian, Mr. Long, and the late Larry LaFever, for looking at me and treating me as the person I would become when I was a lost, derelict teenager. You gave me confidence, and for that I am forever grateful.

Mike Paton, Kelly Knight, and Mark O'Donnell, for succeeding Don and me in EOS Worldwide, and allowing us to pursue our next passions.

My Virtual CEO support team, Lisa Pisano, Kristen Froehlich, and Amy Powell, for keeping everything running like a Swiss watch.

All of the people in the EOS community, the EOS Worldwide leadership team and teammates, and the EOS Implementers. You are putting a real dent in the universe. Thanks for your commitment to the cause and for continuing to put the love in it.

All of my EOS clients, thanks for more than twenty amazing years. I still love every session with you.

James Redfield, for pinging my soul for the first time with your book, *The Celestine Prophecy*.

Rob's Family, Friends, Mentors, and Teachers

Emily, you are the most loving, thoughtful, patient, and caring person I know. You've always supported everything and anything I wanted to do in my life. Never once have I felt pressured or held back. Even when I am squirmy. I love you!

Will, you have a maturity beyond your years, yet you still have that kid-like quality. You recognized early in life to follow your heart. You are thoughtful, humble, hardworking, and loving. I cherish every moment I spend with you. I love you!

Francie, you have made me laugh your entire life. You are creative, smart, independent, caring, and loving. Every time I see your name pop up on my phone, my heart beats with love, and I'm grateful you share all of your daily adventures with me. I love you, Sweets!

My parents, Carol Rozich and Bob Dube´, you've always been there for me, and I'm grateful for the two of you. Your presence in my life shaped me into the person I am today, and I would not change a thing. Your spouses, Bob Rozich and Ruth Dube´, are special people. Cece Johnston, you are so smart and wise. My sister, Michelle Hare, and my brother, Drew Dube´, I love talking and being with the two of you. If only we were neighbors! It is such a gift to know that we are always there for each other (unless you need my help moving, in which case I won't be!). I love you all!

My brother by another mother, Joel Pearlman. Having you and your family in my life is the most unique and special relationship. Thank you for always being my biggest fan, for your constant support, for listening, and for always saying what needs to be said. We are forever connected. I love you!

Jeffery Kaftan, carpe diem! My vision, running, and biking buddy. You are much more than those things to me . . . there is only one Jigggy, that is for sure! You help me see the world in different ways. I'm grateful for your support, your practicality, and your curiosity. Our time together and support for each other goes beyond our friendship. I love you!

Josh Britton, without you, my life would be much different. Our deep conversations about what and how things could be at imageOne changed the course of my life. You are a special friend to me and an amazing leader of the team there. Thank you for asking me to meet for coffee all those years ago, and I'm excited to be on this journey with you.

Gino Wickman, my friend, mentor, and business partner. I had a pretty darn good life going (ha)! Working with you closely has raised my understanding of building a successful business. I love that we are yin/yang and that you are who you are. You are a lifelong learner, and it's inspiring. You are also one of the world's greatest teachers, and you're just getting started. Writing this book with you was fun . . . challenging, but fun! Most of all, I cherish our friendship. It is beyond special and deep. I mean deep. I'm grateful to you, and I love you!

Anese Cavanaugh, I cherish our daily conversations. Emmy Georgeson, your curiosity is a gift to this world. Patricia Karpas, I don't know what I would do without our conversations, our hikes, Milo, our meals together, and your presence at the Do Nothing retreat. Hamsa Daher, I could talk to you for hours nonstop. You are an inspiration to me. Heather Zara, you are a beautiful soul and on the right path. I'm humbled to be on it with you. Janet Solyntjes, thank you for teaching me to be a good student and not to take practice too seriously but to take it seriously.

Our clients, thank you for joining us on this journey, your passion for learning, and allowing us to do this work with you.

My mentors, guides, and friends, Cindy Banchy, Bo Burlingham, Mel Gravely, Dr. Ha Vinh Tho, Rachel Henk, Ryan Henry, Pat Hobby, Thupten Jinpa, Jon Kabat-Zinn, Bud Kirchner, Jack Kornfield, Ashish Kulshrestha, Kristen Masi, Kris Maynard, Michele McHall, Michael McKinney, Hai Nguyen, Laurel Romanella, LeAnne Romo, Sharon Salzburg, Jordan Scharg, Dr. David Seel, Craig Simmons, Paul Spiegelman, Jack Stack, Donna Rockwell, Debra Silverman, Ryan Tansom, Cindy Vuu, Ari Weinzweig, and Mem + Pep (RIP). I love you all!

Contributors

Kristen Froehlich, we are grateful for your unwavering support, which not only kept the writing of this book on track but also ensured our company, The 10 Disciplines, ran smoothly. Your calm demeanor, grace, and steadiness has been lifesaving!

Story contributors: Dan Cornwell, Nathen Fox, Ron Harrell, Josh Holtzman, Patricia Karpas, Brett Kaufman, Nate Klemp, PhD, Dr. Jim Lewerenz, Jillian Lorenz, Justin Maust, Meg Mayhugh, Randy McDougal, Michael McKinney, Denver Nguyen, Mark O'Donnell, Philip Pfeifer, Curt Rager, Eric Rieger, Lynn Rousseau, Joe Stewart, Mike Sullivan, Roderick Walker, Daniel White, and Ginny Wood.

Manuscript readers: Kevin Armstrong, David Bowman, Anese Cavanaugh, Del Collins, Dan Cornwell, Bud Kirchner, Nate Klemp, PhD, Ron Harrell, Keith Jacoby, Brett Kaufman, Kelly Knight, Jillian Lorenz, Rachel Lebowitz, Brandon Marken, Justin Maust, Michael McKinney, Keith Meadows, Michael Morse, Mark O'Donnell, Philip Pfeifer, Curt Rager, Eric Rieger, Lynn Rousseau, Ken Seneff, Mike Sullivan, Roderick Walker, Daniel White, Nathen Fox, and Thomas Wesner.

Other contributors: Our literary agent, Matthew Carnicelli of Carnicelli Literary Management; our editor, John Paine of John Paine Editorial Services; our researcher and fact checker, Veronica Maddocks; Glenn Yeffeth, our publisher; and the team at BenBella Books.

ABOUT THE AUTHORS

An entrepreneur since the age of twenty-one, **Gino Wickman** has always had an obsession for learning what makes businesses and entrepreneurs thrive. He is the author of the bestselling, award-winning book *Traction*, along with six other titles, which together have sold over 2 million copies. He is the creator of EOS® (The Entrepreneurial Operating System®), and founder of EOS Worldwide, one of the largest business coaching companies in the world. There are over 200,000 companies using the EOS tools. These tools help entrepreneurial leaders run a better business, get better control, have better life balance, and gain more traction. After decades of helping entrepreneurs succeed in their outer world, he is now focusing on helping them succeed in their inner world, enabling them to make an even bigger impact while experiencing more fulfillment and peace.

Rob Dube is the cofounder of imageOne, Visionary and CEO of The 10 Disciplines, and cofounder and podcast host of *Entrepreneurial Leap*. He is also the author of *donothing*, host of the Do Nothing retreat, and host of the *Leading with Genuine Care* podcast. Through his work, Rob challenges business leaders and entrepreneurs to look inward with mindfulness and meditation by sharing his own mindful leadership journey.